Who Am I?

Who Am I?

Discovery by Personal Revelation

PAUL BRYAN

RESOURCE *Publications* • Eugene, Oregon

WHO AM I?
Discovery by Personal Revelation

Resource Publications
An Imprint of Wipf and Stock Publishers
199 W. 8th Ave., Suite 3
Eugene, OR 97401

www.wipfandstock.com

PAPERBACK ISBN: 979-8-3852-7739-1
HARDCOVER ISBN: 979-8-3852-7740-7
EBOOK ISBN: 979-8-3852-7741-4

VERSION NUMBER 03/26/26

Contents

PART E | SPIRITUAL GIFTS

PART F | ASSESSING WHO YOU ARE

Acknowledgments

I CAN'T EXPRESS IN words my appreciation for those who worked alongside me during the writing of this book. They have spent many hours reviewing, editing, and providing invaluable feedback to help make this book what it is. Their personal relationship with God and knowledge of the Bible were essential to this end. My wife, Linda, was stalwart in her assistance as she reviewed every chapter.

Introduction

NATURE AND PURPOSE OF BOOK

THIS BOOK WILL HELP you discover who God created you to be and how He is working in your life to form you into the person He desires. You will examine various ways through which He is doing this.

Remember that you have been wonderfully created (Psalm 139:13–18) because God loves you and wants you to spend eternity with Him. That's why He is the Divine Potter, continually shaping and molding you.

MAJOR THEMES

The major themes in this book include the following:

- God gave you a specific natural temperament at physical birth
- Discover what God is doing to shape you
- Discover your natural and spiritual natures that determine who you are
- When you are born-again, you are a new creation in Christ
- Learn that the Holy Spirit gave you spiritual gifts at your spiritual birth
- Take assessments to reveal pieces that form the puzzle of your life
- Review cross-references to understand how natural temperaments and spiritual gifts work together to reveal who you are
- Put all this together in your Profile for a picture of who you are

You Can Find God in This Book

This book will demonstrate that the God of the Bible exists, cares about you, loves you, is available to you, and wants an eternal relationship with you. How exciting it is to know that the supernatural God who created the universe loves you and wants you to spend eternity with Him!

Construction of this Book

Created for Learning

Special Attention
Pay particular attention when you see the following words followed by a colon: Note, Important, and Reminder. They provide explanations and other information to help you understand the text.

Assessments, Cross-References, and Profile

This book is designed to help you discover who God created you to be and how you have developed over time. The assessments and cross-references provide opportunities for this discovery. You enter the results of these into the Profile at the end of the book. The Profile provides a single resource to refer to in the future.

Note: For those unfamiliar with the Bible, I use a standard format for denoting Scripture references. For example, Matthew 28:18–20 refers to the New Testament book of Matthew, the 28th chapter, and verses 18–20 within that chapter. The Bible version is included with the Scripture, such as "NET" (New English Translation).

Additional Books

The author has written two additional Christian non-fiction books you may find interesting. *Unraveling Creation and Evolution through Science and the Bible, Exploring Mysteries, Facts, Theories, and Myths* will help you understand why the sciences support the biblical creation account and disprove the various theories of evolution. If you want to discover more about the God of the Bible, I suggest our first book, *Who Is This God? A Handbook for*

Life with Him. Both books can be purchased from all major online bookstores (Amazon, Barnes and Noble, and more).

PART A

Journey of Discovery

1.

You Are Complicated

WHO AM I? HOW DID I GET THIS WAY?

HAVE YOU HEARD someone say, "I am just a simple person." If so, you will learn that people are not simple at all. In fact, people are complicated in every way.

> You made all the delicate, inner parts of my body and knit me together in my mother's womb. Thank You for making me so wonderfully complex! Your workmanship is marvelous—how well I know it. You watched me as I was being formed in utter seclusion, as I was woven together in the dark of the womb. You saw me before I was born. Every day of my life was recorded in Your book. Every moment was laid out before a single day had passed. (Psalm 139:13–16 NLT)

DIVINE POTTER AND THE CLAY

The Divine Potter is the Father God of the Bible. Just as a human potter creates whatever image He wants from a formless lump of clay, so the Divine Potter created humankind in the way He wanted.

> And yet, O LORD, You are our Father. We are the clay, and You are the potter. We all are formed by Your hand. (Isaiah 64:8 NLT)

You Are Complicated Mold

You are the most complicated creation of God. He is continually molding people by a unique combination of the following:

- Natural temperament
- Natural gifts and talents
- Spiritual gifts
- Education
- Life experiences
- And more

You are God's most complicated creation.

Temperament Introduction

Every person is born physically with a natural temperament. When they are born-again, the Holy Spirit empowers them with spiritual gifts that complement their natural temperament. In other words, a certain temperament is most effective with specific spiritual gifts. For example, a Christian with the gift of service might have the Doer temperament.

Some fundamental aspects of natural temperaments follow:

- People are born with a particular temperament at physical birth
- Their basic temperament does not change
- Their temperament determines how they view and respond to people and the world
- Their temperament determines how well they naturally work on teams and with people
- Their temperament determines what they naturally prefer to do and enjoy the most

Spiritual Gifts Introduction

Every born-again believer is given spiritual gifts that help equip them to carry out the mission of Christ's church.

> So that the body of Christ *[Christians]* may be built up until we all reach unity in the faith and in the knowledge of the Son of God and become mature, attaining to the whole measure of the fullness of Christ. (Ephesians 4:12–13 NIV, author's emphasis)

When each believer does their part, the body of Christ is most effective in fulfilling the mission of the church.

> He makes the whole body fit together perfectly. As each part does its own special work, it helps the other parts grow, so that the whole body is healthy and growing and full of love. (Ephesians 4:16 NLT)

When God leads believers to serve Him and others, all three persons of the Trinity will be involved.

> There are different kinds of spiritual gifts, but the same *Spirit* is the source of them all. There are different kinds of service, but we serve the same *Lord*. God works in different ways, but it is the same *God* who does the work in all of us. (1 Corinthians 12:4–6 NLT, author's emphasis)

DISCOVERY: WHO AM I?

This book is about discovering how God is continually molding you into the person He desires. The assessments and cross-references provide opportunities for this discovery. You enter the results of these into the Profile at the end of the book.

Assessments

The following assessments are included:

- Temperament
- Natural talents and gifts
- Motivation gifts

- Experience and education
- Spiritual maturity
- Ministry passion
- Ministry availability

Cross-References

God enables your natural temperament and spiritual gifts to work together. The cross-references provide a picture of this.

The following cross-references are included:

- Temperament and spiritual gifts
- Temperament and ministry
- Spiritual gifts and ministry

Profile

Each assessment incorporates the changes and transformations that occurred up to the point of the assessment. The results can be noted on the Profile at the end of the book. This provides a single, convenient place to review the information you've created, helping you understand who the Divine Potter is molding you to be.

CREATED BY GOD FOR A PURPOSE

You were created by God to fulfill His purposes for your life and His Kingdom. That is good news!

The following Scriptures describe this:

1. You are God's mold, not your own

> Who are you, a mere human being, to argue with God? Should the thing that was created say to the one who created it, "Why have you made me like this?" (Romans 9:20 NLT)

2. When God created you, He knew what you would become.

> Thank you for making me so wonderfully complex! Your workmanship is marvelous—how well I know it. You watched me as I was being formed in utter seclusion, as I was woven together in the dark of the womb. You saw me before I was born. Every day of my life was recorded in your book. Every moment was laid out before a single day had passed. (Psalm 139:14–16 NLT)

3. You were designed by God for a purpose.

> For we are God's workmanship, created in Christ Jesus to do good works, which God prepared in advance for us to do. (Ephesians 2:10 NIV)
>
> Bring all who claim Me as their God, for I have made them for My glory. It was I who created them. (Isaiah 43:7 NLT)

Be Honest

Remember, it's about you, and not what someone else thinks of you. So, be honest with yourself as you embark on this journey of discovery. You were created out of the heart of the Father's love. How wonderful it is to know that you have been molded and equipped for a purpose in His world!

PART B

Nature of God and People

2.

Three-Fold Nature of God

To HELP YOU understand who you are, you must have a basic understanding of who your Creator God is. This is because you are created in His image.

GOD OF THE BIBLE IS THE TRINITY

The God of the Bible is the Triune God, consisting of the Father, the Son, Jesus Christ, and the Holy Spirit. Each is equally divine and fully God in their essential being and nature. The image of God given to humankind comes from their nature. The unfathomable greatness of God can be seen in the triune nature of their existence as one God.

The following verse states that the God of the Bible is one God:

> Jesus answered, "The foremost is, 'Hear, o Israel! The LORD our God is one LORD'" (Mark 12:29 NASB)

This nature of God is referred to as the "Triune God" or the "Trinity." These terms don't appear in the Bible. Biblical scholars created them to identify the unity of one God existing in three persons.

We see the Trinity mentioned in the New Testament:

> Jesus told his disciples, "Therefore, go and make disciples of all the nations, baptizing them in the name of the Father and the Son and the Holy Spirit." (Matthew 28:19 NLT)

> May the grace of the Lord Jesus Christ, and the love of God, and the fellowship of the Holy Spirit be with you all. (2 Corinthians 13:14 NIV)

THREE-FOLD NATURE OF GOD

Three-Fold Divine Nature of God

Let's look at Scripture to view the three-fold nature of God. This nature consists of a soul, a spirit, and a physical form. I think you will agree that each person of God has a soul and spirit as part of their divine nature. But there are differences in their physical natures.

Each person of the Trinity has a three-fold nature.

The following is a summary of my understanding of Scripture regarding the divine three-fold nature of each person of God. Only a physical form or material substance is different for each of them.

- Soul: Each person of God has a soul
- Spirit: Each person of God has a spirit
- Physical form or material substance: This is different for each person of God

Soul

Throughout the Bible, we see each person of God exhibiting characteristics of a soul. These are similar characteristics we see in people since they are made in God's image.

I believe God's soul consists of the following:

- Emotions (feelings)
- Will
- Reasoning/Thinking

- Memories
- Conscience (morality)

Note: The human soul is made like God's soul, but is not divine. It's the human soul that was corrupted at the fall of Adam and Eve. This corrupted image conceals the original soul.

Spirit

Each person of God must have a spirit and be a spiritual being.

Note: I believe it's the human spirit, made in the image of God, that makes people unique among all other creatures.

Physical Body

Scripture clearly states that Jesus Christ has a physical body. He ascended to Heaven with it:

> Notice that it says "He ascended." This clearly means that Christ also descended to our lowly world. (Ephesians 4:9 NLT)

We know, however, that the Holy Spirit does not have a material, physical body (John 3:6–8). Scripture says that the Father God is a spirit and therefore appears to lack physical substance.

3.

Three-Fold Nature of People

In this chapter, you will learn that God created people on Day Six when He made all land-based creatures. You will learn that He created people with a three-fold nature of a spirit, a soul, and a physical body.

> God said, "Let the land produce living creatures according to their kinds: cattle, creeping things, and wild animals, each according to its kind." It was so. God made the wild animals according to their kinds, the cattle according to their kinds, and all the creatures that creep along the ground according to their kinds. God saw that it was good. Then God said, "Let us make humankind in our image, after our likeness, so they may rule over the fish of the sea and the birds of the air, over the cattle, and over all the earth, and over all the creatures that move on the earth." God created humankind in his own image, in the image of God he created them, male and female he created them. (Genesis 1:24–27 NET)
>
> The Hebrew word for "image" is *tselem*, which means a resemblance or representative figure, such as a likeness or representation.

PEOPLE CREATED WITH A THREE-FOLD NATURE

The three-fold nature of people is clearly seen in the New Testament:

> Now may the God of peace himself make you completely holy and may your *spirit* and *soul* and *body* be kept entirely blameless at

> the coming of our Lord Jesus Christ. (1 Thessalonians 5:23 NET, author's emphasis)

HUMAN SOUL

The physical body is the exterior shell in which the soul and spirit reside. Therefore, the real person is on the inside. We talk about a person's personality that reflects the individual's uniqueness. No two persons are exactly alike.

The human soul is made in the image of God, so it consists of the same things as God's soul:

- Emotions (feelings)
- Will
- Reasoning/Thinking
- Memories
- Conscience (morality)

HUMAN SPIRIT: UNIQUE TO PEOPLE

Many characteristics of the human soul are visible in animals, especially in primates such as apes and chimpanzees. However, there is no scientific evidence that animals are self-aware and therefore possess a conscience. Animals also do not have a spirit enabling them to commune and communicate with God as born-again Christians can do.

Purpose of the Spirit in People

I believe the purpose of the human spirit is to enable people to commune and communicate with their Creator God. However, they lost this ability after Adam and Eve's rebellion. These spiritual abilities are only restored when people accept Jesus Christ as their Savior and Lord. At that moment, the Holy Spirit comes to live with them and they are born-again.

The spirit is unique to humans among all created animals

The following are some Scriptures that say the Holy Spirit speaks to the born-again human spirit to reveal the things of God:

> That is what the Scriptures mean when they say, "No eye has seen, no ear has heard, and no mind has imagined what God has prepared for those who love Him." But it was to us that God revealed these things by His Spirit. For His Spirit searches out everything and shows us God's deep secrets. For who among men knows the things of a man except the man's spirit within him? So too, no one knows the things of God except the Spirit of God. Now we have not received the spirit of the world, but the Spirit who is from God, so that we may know the things that are freely given to us by God. And we speak about these things, not with words taught us by human wisdom, but with those taught by the Spirit, explaining spiritual things to spiritual people. (1 Corinthians 2:9–13 NLT)

Human Spirit Is Dead to God without the Holy Spirit

Ephesians 2:5–6 says that non-believers are dead to God due to their unforgiven sins. But what is dead? Not their physical body nor their soul. They were physically alive, and they could think and feel, so it was their spirit that was dead to God. If something is dead, it cannot function. It needs resurrection to become alive and functional. I believe the Holy Spirit makes the human spirit alive to God at the moment they are born-again. They then become spiritual beings.

> Even though we were dead because of our sins, He gave us life when He raised Christ from the dead. (It is only by God's grace that you have been saved!) For He raised us from the dead along with Christ and seated us with Him in the heavenly realms because we are united with Christ Jesus. (Ephesians 2:5–6 NLT)

HUMAN PHYSICAL BODY

Purpose of the Human Body

God gave humankind a physical body to enable them to live and work in the physical world He created.

We see this in the following verses:

> For the LORD is God, and He created the heavens and earth and put everything in place. He made the world to be lived in, not to be a place of empty chaos. (Isaiah 45:18 NLT)

> The LORD God took the man and put him in the garden of Eden to work it and keep it. (Genesis 2:15 ESV)

PART C

The Natural Person

4.

Natural Needs of People

In this chapter, you will examine the nature of human beings as expressed through their needs, including spiritual needs. It provides another perspective on who God has created you to be.

Note: People did not have needs before the fall of Adam and Eve since they were made in the perfect image of God.

HUMAN NEEDS

There are needs that are common to all people, regardless of where they were born, gender, ethnicity, culture, and so on.

Note: Some other analyses of needs include cultural needs that are acquired from an individual's culture. We will not review these, as they can vary widely across people groups and cultures.

Human Needs Revealed

So, what is a human need? How is it different from a want?

Human needs and wants arose as part of the corrupted human nature. Human needs exist for everyone, but not everyone will experience the same needs. Some needs can only be fulfilled through your own efforts, while others can be fulfilled through other people.

The following are lists of some of the most important human needs. These are not all-inclusive lists.

Survival needs:

- Water
- Food
- Shelter
- Warmth
- Sleep

Psychological needs:

- Touch
- Hope
- Self-esteem
- Rest
- Respect
- Love

Social needs:

- Interaction
- Acceptance
- Reinforcement
- Affection and love
- Community
- Trust
- Loyalty

Spiritual Needs

I believe there are also spiritual needs required for a healthy life. Spiritual needs point people to their need for salvation and eternal life with God. God created people for relationship. This means they are wired with needs for a spiritual relationship with the God of the Bible.

The following are some spiritual needs that only the God of the Bible can fulfill:

- Redemption/Salvation
- Removal of all sin and its consequences
- Personal relationship with God
- Trust in God
- Hope
- Peace of soul
- Joy of the Lord
- Eternal destiny with God

People who have not trusted Christ for salvation may experience the following needs:

- Hopelessness
- Loneliness
- Lack of eternal purpose for life
- Trust in self only (instead of God)
- Dissatisfaction with life
- Excessiveness

How do you feel about the spiritual needs? Do they scare or comfort you?

5.

Stop Lying to Yourself

THIS CHAPTER DESCRIBES living free from the false guilt, shameful thoughts, and self-destructive excesses that can plague people, including some born-again followers of Jesus Christ.

LIES YOU TELL YOURSELF

People tell themselves lies all the time. Why do they do this? Because they have accepted lies from various sources and don't know how to counter them. Lies are accepted first in our minds. They move deeper into the soul as we embrace them as our own. Lies can wound people's hearts and minds.

What lies do you tell yourself?

Important: You can become the victor or remain a victim; the choice is yours. Don't let lies define who you are.

Sources of lies may include the following:

- Other people (including parents, friends, and marriage partner)
- World and its sins
- Teachers and leaders
- False religious beliefs

Common Lies People Tell Themselves

There are many common lies people tell themselves. You may find you have believed some of these about yourself.

The following are examples of lies people tell themselves:

- You are not worthy to be a human being
- You will never amount to anything
- You are ugly
- No one will ever love you
- You will fail at everything you do
- Why not just give up
- Your life is not worth living
- You must be perfect in everything
- Your parents are the reason you are this way
- God must not love you
- You need to earn God's love
- Value of your life is determined by how well you perform

Only Truth Overcomes Lies

All lies must be overcome with truth from God. He is truth by His very nature, and all that He says and does is true. You can learn about His truth and love for you from the Bible.

> Lead me by Your truth and teach me, for You are the God who saves me. All day long I put my hope in You. (Psalm 25:5 NLT)
>
> But when he, the Spirit of truth, comes, he will guide you into all truth. For he will not speak on his own authority, but will speak whatever he hears, and will tell you what is to come. (John 16:13 NET)

RENEW YOUR MIND

The Bible is God's living and powerful Word (Hebrews 4:12). Born-again believers must use it accurately and consistently so the Holy Spirit can renew their minds and hearts.

> Let the Spirit renew your thoughts and attitudes. (Ephesians 4:23 NLT)

God tells you in the following Scripture how to renew your mind:

> But now is the time to get rid of anger, rage, malicious behavior, slander, and dirty language. Don't lie to each other, for you have stripped off your old sinful nature and all its wicked deeds. Put on your new nature, and be renewed as you learn to know your Creator and become like Him. . . . Since God chose you to be the holy people He loves, you must clothe yourselves with tenderhearted mercy, kindness, humility, gentleness, and patience. Make allowance for each other's faults, and forgive anyone who offends you. Remember, the Lord forgave you, so you must forgive others. Above all, clothe yourselves with love, which binds us all together in perfect harmony. And let the peace that comes from Christ rule in your hearts. For as members of one body you are called to live in peace. And always be thankful. Let the message about Christ, in all its richness, fill your lives.Teach and counsel each other with all the wisdom He gives. Sing psalms and hymns and spiritual songs to God with thankful hearts. And whatever you do or say, do it as a representative of the Lord Jesus, giving thanks through Him to God the Father. (Colossians 3:8–17 NLT)

God's living word is transforming the renewed mind and heart of a Christian into the nature of Christ.

6.

Your Natural Temperament

AT PHYSICAL BIRTH, God gave you the strengths and abilities of a specific temperament to enable you to fulfill His purposes.

God gave you a natural temperament at physical birth.

The following Scripture says that God created you for His purposes:

> Thank you for making me so wonderfully complex! Your workmanship is marvelous—how well I know it. You watched me as I was being formed in utter seclusion, as I was woven together in the dark of the womb. You saw me before I was born. Every day of my life was recorded in your book. Every moment was laid out before a single day had passed. (Psalm 139:14–16 NLT)

Aspects of a Temperament

Some fundamental aspects of temperaments follow:

- You are born with your specific temperament at physical birth
- Your basic temperament does not change (your personality may change)
- Your temperament determines how you view and respond to people and the world with which you interact

- Your temperament determines how well you naturally work on teams and with people
- Your temperament determines what you naturally prefer to do and enjoy the most
- Your temperament has nothing to do with your intelligence, education, character, or emotional maturity
- You can learn to change your behavior to help you overcome the weaknesses of your temperament
- You can also develop and mature your temperament strengths

Note: Don't confuse your temperament with learned behaviors, which you develop over time. Many factors, including your temperament, shape your personality.

Each temperament is best suited for certain types of responsibility, service, and ministry:

- Relator: people-centric
- Doer: task-centric
- Thinker: detailed and planning-centric
- Influencer: motivation-centric

CHARACTERISTICS OF FOUR TEMPERAMENTS

The following pages describe characteristics of the four temperaments. These characteristics include strengths and weaknesses.

Reminder: Many people are a blend of two or more temperaments. One temperament often prevails as the predominant temperament in a blend. This can be identified because it will be the temperament from which a person initially responds to people and life events. Understanding a temperament's weaknesses can help confirm its predominance in a person.

DOER TEMPERAMENT

The Doer is the task-oriented temperament.

The following represents the typical individual with a high Doer temperament.

Typical Doer Strengths/Abilities:

- Decisions made quickly
- Quick results with minimal details
- Find solutions to problems
- Be in charge of work activities and results
- Trusts own skills to accomplish work
- Solving difficult and challenging problems
- Prefer to work alone (not a team player)
- Strong-willed to endure difficulties

Typical Doer Weaknesses/Areas of Improvement:

- Don't consider the feelings or needs of others
- Lack patience for those who cannot keep pace with them
- Impulsive, so doesn't see risks to people and project success
- Don't accurately assess abilities to get work done
- Don't plan or want details since these slow down getting things done quickly
- Don't want boundaries and restrictions for themselves or the work
- Too high expectations of the capabilities and work results of others
- Believe their perspective on the work is always better than that of others
- Do it their way or get out of the way

Likely Motivation Gifts: Prophecy, giving, administration, or service.

INFLUENCER TEMPERAMENT

The Influencer is the public speaker, the champion temperament.

Note: Interwoven into the Influencer's God-given nature are Relator and Doer temperament characteristics.

The following represents the typical individual with a high Influencer temperament.

Typical Influencer Strengths/Abilities:

- Visionary with creative ideas
- Positive and optimistic attitude toward work and life
- Enjoy people and relate easily to them
- Appreciated by people for their vision
- Words come easily to them
- Primarily motivated to help groups
- Provide an entertaining atmosphere
- Hospitable and engaging

Typical Influencer Weaknesses/Areas of Improvement:

- Don't complete tasks
- Anticipated results may not match reality
- Don't judge capabilities correctly, so that work can be incomplete
- Talk excessively and dominate conversations
- Lack of planning results in impulsive reactions
- Inability to handle finances wisely
- Sees people as resources needed to get things done

Likely Motivation Gifts: Giving or exhortation.

RELATOR TEMPERAMENT

The Relator is the people-person temperament.

Note: The Relator loves to be with people, individually or in small groups.

The following represents the typical individual with a high Relator temperament.

Typical Relator Strengths/Abilities:

- Supportive of others
- Agreeable with others
- Loyal to those they support
- Self-control in difficult situations
- Consistency in behavior
- Good listener
- Perform established work routines (don't like change)

Typical Relator Weaknesses/Areas of Improvement:

- Resist change (can feel insecure with change)
- Deadlines not important
- Overly lenient with others
- Procrastinate getting things done
- Indecisive in decision-making
- Hold a grudge when hurt deeply
- Overly possessive of people close to them
- Lack of initiative in making changes

Likely Motivation Gifts: Mercy; possibly exhortation or teaching.

THINKER TEMPERAMENT

The Thinker is the detailed, analytical temperament. The quality control temperament.

The following represents the typical individual with a high Thinker temperament.

Typical Thinker Strengths/Abilities:

- Detailed and thorough analyses
- Organization and orderliness
- Conscientious in doing what is right and best
- Quality of work/precision (it must be right)
- Personal discipline in work processes and life
- Treating others with dignity and diplomacy
- Desire to improve work and organizational performance

Typical Thinker Weaknesses/Areas of Improvement:

- Indecisive in decision-making (analysis paralysis)
- Loose big picture with excessive attention to detail
- Inflexible, since work must get done the way they want
- Avoid conflict due to low self-esteem
- Resist change and anything new
- Prefer limited responsibilities to focus on work quality
- Lack a positive view of life and work since nothing can be perfect

Likely Motivation Gifts: Teaching or administration; possibly exhortation.

EXAMPLES OF TEMPERAMENTS IN THE BIBLE

The following are examples of people in the New Testament and their possible temperament:

- Doer: Peter (Acts 2); Barnabas (Acts 11:22–30; 1 Corinthians 9:6); Paul (Book of Acts)

- Relator: John (Book of 1 John); Paul (Books of Acts and Philippians)
- Influencer: Apollos (Acts 18:24–28)
- Thinker: Paul (Acts 26:24)

Note: The Apostle Paul was likely a four-way blend of Doer, Relator, Influencer, and Thinker.

SUMMARY OF KEY TEMPERAMENT CHARACTERISTICS

Following is a summary of key characteristics for each of the four temperaments. Consider which characteristics align with your lifestyle, behavior, and motivation to determine your temperament. (Most people are a temperament blend.)

Doer	*Relator*
1. Task-oriented	1. People-oriented
2. Loves a challenge	2. Loves to spend time one-on-one with a person
3. Great problem solver	3. Sensitive to people's feelings
4. Wants to get things done now	4. Wants to take time to build a relationship with a person
5. Not sensitive to people's feelings	5. Is detailed oriented as it relates to people and their feelings
6. Often sees people as a nuisance when they want to get things done	6. Does not like other details or to plan ahead
7. Does not like detail or to plan ahead	7. Very loyal to people
8. Takes things as they come	8. Very compassionate
9. Does not feel they really need people	9. Likes boundaries
10. Does not like boundaries	10. "Give me the time to spend with people"
11. "Leave me alone and let me do it"	

Influencer	*Thinker*
1. Task and people-oriented	1. Detail-oriented
2. Desires to influence people to accomplish tasks	2. Not task or people-oriented
3. Sees people as resources needed to get things done	3. Anaylitcal
4. Not sensitive to people's feelings	4. Likes to plan ahead
5. Focus on groups of people, not individuals	5. Orderly with good organzation skills
6. Very positive	6. Does things in sequential order
7. Cheerleader for group	7. Not sensitive to people's feelings
8. Needs to be appreciated	8. Prone to depression
9. Likes to help	9. Can have low self-esteem
10. Does not like detail or to plan ahead	10. Quality-control person; Wants to do it right the first time
11. Does not like boundaries	11. Can get lost in detail and delay getting things done
12. "Give me an opportunity to tell people about it"	12. Likes boundaries and structure
	13. "If I'm going to do it, I want the time to do it right the first time"

STORIES ABOUT TEMPERAMENTS

Each of the following stories exemplifies the strengths and weaknesses of a temperament. I am using fictitious names (except the fifth story, which is about me).

Story One (Doer and Relator). Tom is a Doer, and his wife, Sue, is a Relator. Their differences were so enormous that they were considering divorce. Even their five girls suggested divorce so there would be peace. (Tom and Sue are Christians.) Tom was the classic Doer who wanted to be left alone to focus on tasks, making quick decisions with little planning. He wanted to see change now. However, he did not consider others' feelings and lacked patience. Sue was the classic Relator who wanted to spend uninterrupted, quality time with her husband and friends. She was loyal and supportive. However, she did not like change and was resistant to being pressured into it. Deadlines and quick results were not as important as people's feelings.

When Tom and Sue attended a class I taught on temperaments, they each saw themselves in the strengths and weaknesses of their temperament and that of their spouse. They were stunned to realize they could overcome their weaknesses and learn to appreciate the other's temperament. They rediscovered their first love for each other and began rebuilding their marriage.

Story Two (Influencer). Pastor Samual is a good man and a solid Christian in his late forties. He has been preaching for nearly twenty years. As I watch him in various situations, I recognize both his Influencer temperament strengths and weaknesses. In fact, he represents the clearest picture of an Influencer I have ever met. He can create visions people want to follow because they trust him. He is verbally articulate and persuasive in his optimistic approach to ministry and the church's future. People easily catch his vision. However, he tends to oversell his ideas and underestimate the church's and people's capabilities to achieve the vision. His lack of detailed planning and rush to get things done led to the failure of a prior church project. He disregards this failure as he encourages the church to accept his next vision.

Story Three (Relator). We have known Mary for several decades. She is the classic Relator. She loves being around people and enjoys conversing with them. Like Sue, she has the tender strengths that enable her to be a loyal and supportive friend. She also dislikes change, can procrastinate, and prefers consistency in her life.

When she was first learning about temperaments in a class I taught, she found it difficult to understand the motives and behavior of her church's senior pastor, who was a Doer temperament. She felt herself in emotional conflict about this. Several decades later, she appreciates the strengths of her current young Doer pastor and accepts him as he is. She knows that he will grow and master his temperament over time, just as she did.

Story Four (Thinker). I have known Bud for twenty years. He is a mature and honorable man of God, gifted in teaching the Bible. As a result, many people have grown in their Christian faith. If you knew him and read the strengths and weaknesses of the Thinker temperament, you would clearly see a picture of Bud. He is studious, analytical, and detail-oriented, with a passion for getting things right. Yet, he also exhibits the typical weaknesses of the Thinker temperament. He can be inflexible, resist change, and prefers limited responsibilities.

Story Five. I am a Doer/Thinker temperament blend. I have the strengths and weaknesses of both temperaments. I am not naturally people-oriented. However, God continues to reshape me as a follower of Jesus. I am now more than what I once was. Even though I struggle at times to want to be with people, I find that the Holy Spirit imparts His love for them to me. I am learning how to love and care about people. In fact, our adult Sunday School teacher recently told the class that I say I am not a people-person, yet I spend more time talking with people before class than anyone else.

Note: The Holy Spirit can help you overcome your temperament weaknesses if you ask. But you have to be willing to change! And change for many people is not an easy path.

7.

Gifts, But Not Spiritual Gifts

Just as people are born with a natural temperament, they are also born with natural gifts and talents. These interact with their temperament to help determine how they relate to people and life.

The list below includes gifts not found in the four major lists of spiritual gifts. They are in the Bible, but do not fulfill the fundamental purpose of spiritual gifts, which is to edify, build up, and strengthen Christians spiritually.

The following gifts are found in Scripture:

- Craftsmanship/Artist (Exodus 31:3–4)
- Hospitality (1 Peter 4:9)
- Intercessory prayer (Colossians 4:12–13)
- Writing (1 Timothy 3:14–15)
- Music (Colossians 3:16; 1 Corinthians 14:26)
- Voluntary poverty (2 Corinthians 8:9)
- Celibacy (1 Corinthians 7:7)

Some are natural gifts, such as craftsmanship (using wood, silver, gold, or clay), music, sports, and writing. Others appear to be a special ability given to some Christians to live uniquely according to God's plan, such as celibacy or voluntary poverty.

The following verses describe how God gives people natural gifts and talents for His purposes:

> The LORD spoke to Moses: "See, I have chosen Bezalel son of Uri, the son of Hur, of the tribe of Judah, and I have filled him with the Spirit of God in skill, in understanding, in knowledge, and in all kinds of craftsmanship, to make artistic designs for work with gold, with silver, and with bronze, and with cutting and setting stone, and with cutting wood, to work in all kinds of craftsmanship. Moreover, I have also given him Oholiab son of Ahisamach, of the tribe of Dan, and I have given ability to all the specially skilled, that they may make everything I have commanded you. (Exodus 31:1–6 NET)

CHRISTIANS AND NON-BELIEVERS HAVE THEM

Believers and non-believers alike have natural gifts and talents. Christians can use their natural gifts and talents after they are spiritually born-again to bless God's people. One common example is music. A Christian musician can use their spiritual gift (such as exhortation) with their natural gift for music. How many of us have felt the presence of the Holy Spirit when a believer with the natural gift of music sings or plays an instrument beautifully under the influence of the Holy Spirit!

PART D

The Spiritual Person

8.

You Must Be Born-Again

BORN-AGAIN: WHAT IT REALLY MEANS

My life has never been the same since that day in May 1976 when the Holy Spirit came to live within me. As a result, I have been a born-again follower of Christ for nearly 50 years. Unfortunately, many people, including Christians, don't know what born-again means and how it happens. Many people seem to lack a biblical understanding of the Holy Spirit. And if they don't know who the Holy Spirit is, they likely don't know about being born-again. We don't often hear about Him and our need to be born-again from pastors and Bible study teachers. I also wonder if the term "born-again" is a turn-off for some people? The term may even polarize people within a denomination. I am sure it grieves the Holy Spirit to see this division.

Note: Jesus said that everyone must be born-again to enter the Kingdom of God (John 3:3).

When Does It Happen?

A study of Scripture reveals that being born-again means the Holy Spirit comes to dwell within believers:

> And I will ask the Father, and He will give you another Advocate, who will never leave you. He is the Holy Spirit, who leads into all truth. The world can't receive Him, because it isn't looking for Him

> and doesn't recognize Him. But you know Him, because He lives with you now and later will be in you. (John 14:16–17 NLT)

Jesus said that unless you are born-again, you can't enter the Kingdom of Heaven.

> Jesus said, "I tell you the truth, unless you are born-again, you cannot see the Kingdom of God." "What do You mean?" exclaimed Nicodemus. "How can an old man go back into his mother's womb and be born-again?" Jesus replied, "I assure you, no one can enter the Kingdom of God without being born of water and the Spirit. Humans can reproduce only human life, but the Holy Spirit gives birth to spiritual life. So don't be surprised when I say, 'You must be born- again.'" (John 3:3–7 NLT)

People have a physical birth when they are born into the natural world. (That's when they are given their temperament.) They experience a spiritual birth when they are born spiritually by the Holy Spirit.

> Jesus replied, "I assure you, no one can enter the Kingdom of God without being born of water and the Spirit. Humans can reproduce only human life, but the Holy Spirit gives birth to spiritual life." (John 3:5–6 NLT)

Have you been born-again by accepting Jesus as Savior and Lord?

Born-Again to a Living Hope

New believers receive a living hope when they are born-again. This hope is an assurance, a certainty, that they will live eternally with God. It's living because the Holy Spirit lives within them, empowering and enabling them to enjoy life with the Father, Jesus, and Himself.

> Blessed be the God and Father of our Lord Jesus Christ, who according to His great mercy has caused us to be born-again to a living hope through the resurrection of Jesus Christ from the dead. (1 Peter 1:3 NASB)

Born-Again into God's Eternal Family

When a person is born-again, the Father adopts them into His eternal family. Thus, they become a spiritual child of the Father God and a brother of His Son, Jesus.

> And because we are His children, God has sent the Spirit of His Son into our hearts, prompting us to call out, "Abba, Father." (Galatians 4:6 NLT)

When this occurs, they receive an eternal inheritance as a member of God's family.

> All praise to God, the Father of our Lord Jesus Christ. It is by His great mercy that we have been born-again, because God raised Jesus Christ from the dead. Now we live with great expectation, and we have a priceless inheritance—an inheritance that is kept in heaven for you, pure and undefiled, beyond the reach of change and decay. (1 Peter 1:3–4 NLT)

It's impossible to consistently live the Christian life without being born-again by the Holy Spirit. But it's not the experience of being born-again that's important. Instead, it's having an eternal, living relationship with the Father, Jesus, and the Holy Spirit.

9.

A New Creation in Christ

Consider the earlier question: Who am I? How did I get this way?

The simple answer is that you become a new creation when you are born-again.

> Therefore, if anyone is in Christ, the new creation has come. (2 Corinthians 5:17 NIV)

The Greek word for new used in the above verse (*kainos*) means it's a unique nature that didn't previously exist in you. The Holy Spirit does not simply take the existing self-centered, old nature and modify, improve, or renovate it. If you are a follower of Jesus Christ, you can't live the new Christian life in a way that pleases God with just an improved self-centered old nature. You must be given a new nature that enables you to experience your new spiritual relationship and life with God.

The following verse says that we are to stop living by our self-centered old nature and live by our new Christ-centered nature.

> Don't lie to each other, for you have stripped off your old sinful nature and all its wicked deeds. Put on your new nature, and be renewed as you learn to know your Creator and become like Him. (Colossians 3:9–10 NLT)

BELIEVERS HAVE TWO NATURES

The old and new natures are integral to your being as a new believer. You continue to have a self-centered old nature, but now you also have a Christ-centered new nature. However, you can't live by both natures at the same time. One nature will always dominate and control your thinking, behaviors, and life. The old nature is your default nature because you have lived by it your entire life. As such, it is often your first response to life. It will always have control over you unless you work with the Holy Spirit to retrain yourself to respond from your new nature.

Since you committed your life to Jesus Christ, you want the Holy Spirit and your new nature to control you. You have a choice, but it is not an easy choice to follow.

> Those who live according to the flesh have their minds set on what the flesh desires; but those who live in accordance with the Spirit have their minds set on what the Spirit desires. The mind governed by the flesh is death, but the mind governed by the Spirit is life and peace. The mind governed by the flesh is hostile to God; it does not submit to God's law, nor can it do so. Those who are in the realm of the flesh cannot please God. (Romans 8:5–8 NIV)

Note: Being in the realm of the flesh is another way of saying people are living by their self-centered old nature.

The following verse says you must continually exert a determined effort to obey God and live by the Holy Spirit and your new nature:

> Work hard to show the results of your salvation, obeying God with deep reverence and fear. (Philippians 2:12 NLT)

THE OLD NATURE

When I say your old nature is self-centered, I mean it's focused on what you want rather than on what God wants. You don't naturally submit to Jesus Christ as the One in charge of your life. You always want to be in charge. You rely on your judgment and trust your choices instead of the Holy Spirit. Maybe you are the most loving, caring, compassionate, and giving person in the world. However, you still have a self-centered.

THE NEW NATURE

If you say, "Jesus is Lord of my life!" What should it mean? It means that you sincerely desire Jesus to be in charge of everything. You want Him to help you make decisions that are according to the Father's will. Jesus does this through your new nature and His Spirit, which live within you as a born-again Christian.

In the following verse, "put on the new self" means you must actively participate in this transformative process.

> Put on the new self who is being renewed to a true knowledge according to the image of the One who created him. (Colossians 3:10 NASB)

The following verses describe the fruit of the Spirit, which characterizes your new nature:

> Put on then, as God's chosen ones, holy and beloved, compassionate hearts, kindness, humility, meekness, and patience, bearing with one another and, if one has a complaint against another, forgiving each other; as the Lord has forgiven you, so you also must forgive. And above all these put on love, which binds everything together in perfect harmony. And let the peace of Christ rule in your hearts, to which indeed you were called in one body. And be thankful (Colossians 3:12–15 ESV)

Is the fruit of the Spirit evident in your life?

HOLY SPIRIT NEEDS TO GUIDE YOU

It's essential to continually ask the Holy Spirit to guide your decisions, expectations, motives, and behaviors. However, you must train yourself so that your new nature will mature over time. Just as a baby needs physical food to help it grow physically, you need spiritual food (God's living word) to help you grow spiritually.

> You have been believers so long now that you ought to be teaching others. Instead, you need someone to teach you again the basic things about God's word. You are like babies who need milk and

> cannot eat solid food. For someone who lives on milk is still an infant and doesn't know how to do what is right. Solid food is for those who are mature, who through training have the skill to recognize the difference between right and wrong. (Hebrews 5:12–14 NLT)

Living by your new nature can be a daily battle, but the result brings peace, joy, and fruitfulness in God's Kingdom on Earth.

10.

Transformed by the Spirit

As a follower of Jesus, God gives you a choice about how to live your life. This is known as free will. You may choose to allow the Holy Spirit direct your thinking, motivations, conversations, and behaviors, or allow your comfortable old nature to control you.

The following verses are a reminder of the consequences of these choices:

> For those who live according to the flesh set their minds on the things of the flesh, but those who live according to the Spirit set their minds on the things of the Spirit. For to set the mind on the flesh is death, but to set the mind on the Spirit is life and peace. For the mind that is set on the flesh is hostile to God, for it does not submit to God's law; indeed, it cannot. Those who are in the flesh cannot please God. (Romans 8:5–8 ESV)

HOLY SPIRIT CAN TRANSFORM YOUR HEART AND MIND

Allow the Holy Spirit to transform and control you. In so doing, you will learn to know God's will for you.

> Don't copy the behavior and customs of this world, but let God transform you into a new person by changing the way you think. Then you will learn to know God's will for you, which is good and pleasing and perfect. (Romans 12:2 NLT)

The English word "transformed" comes from the Greek "*metamorphose*." It refers to an ongoing process of progressive change. A caterpillar is an excellent example of metamorphosis. Over time, it's transformed into a beautiful butterfly.

Note: These changes occur on the inside (your mind and heart) before they are visible in your outside behavior.

Allow the Holy Spirit to transform you continually.

THE BODY GROWS OLD, BUT THE SOUL IS RENEWED

In the following verse, the Apostle Paul says that the inner man is renewed even while the physical body grows old.

> Therefore we do not lose heart, but though our outer man is decaying, yet our inner man is being renewed day by day. (2 Corinthians 4:16 NASB)

IF LOVE STOPS GROWING, IT STARTS DYING

Story. Before my wife and I were allowed to be married in our church, we were required to participate in a pre-marriage course led by a pastor of our church. It was practical, covering topics that might later lead to a problematic marriage. It included topics such as financial management, getting along with in-laws, preferred leisure activities, and more. The pastor made a statement I had never heard before: "When love stops growing, it starts dying." Since then, I have often thought about this. I see its applicability to all relationships, including those with your spouse and God. When love for your spouse or God stops growing, it inevitably begins to die.

The following verse says that without God's love, we are nothing:

> And if I have prophecy, and know all mysteries and all knowledge, and if I have all faith so that I can remove mountains, but do not have love, I am nothing. (1 Corinthians 13:2 NET)

DON'T NEGLECT THE HOLY SPIRIT

The following verse says that believers can quench the activity of the Holy Spirit by neglecting to live by His presence and power. This quenching causes the Spirit's life and fruit to diminish and begin to die.

> Do not quench the Spirit. (1 Thessalonians 5:19 NASB)

The Greek word *sbennumi*, translated "quench," means to extinguish something, as one would pour water on a fire to put it out. It can also mean neglecting to provide the fire with the fuel it needs. In other words, neglecting to live a disciplined life controlled by the Spirit will quench His activity within the believer.

The following verse about grieving the Holy Spirit has the same effect on His ability to impart spiritual life and manifest His influences in a believer:

> Do not grieve the Holy Spirit of God, by whom you were sealed for the day of redemption. (Ephesians 4:30 NASB)

The Greek word, *lupeō*, translated "grieve," can mean to sadden or make sorrowful.

Quenching and grieving the Holy Spirit can result in His withdrawing His influence and ceasing to work within believers. The believer's spiritual life and love for God and others wither as they strive to live by their self-centered old nature. Their new nature is thwarted and becomes less expressive as they slip further into their old ways of thinking and behaving.

PART E

Spiritual Gifts

11.

What Spiritual Gifts Are

ALL GIFTS FROM God are free. God does not charge us or expect us to earn them. The gift of salvation is the greatest gift we have from God.

> For by grace you have been saved through faith. And this is not your own doing; it is the gift of God, not a result of works, so that no one may boast. (Ephesians 2:8–9 ESV)

The Father God has also given the gift of the Holy Spirit to live within those who accept Jesus as Savior and Lord.

> I will ask the Father, and he will give you another Helper, to be with you forever, even the Spirit of truth, whom the world cannot receive, because it neither sees him nor knows him. You know him, for he dwells with you and will be in you. (John 14:16–17 ESV)

EVERY CHRISTIAN HAS A SPIRITUAL GIFT

Every born-again Christian has one or more spiritual gifts.

You cannot serve God effectively apart from the Holy Spirit and His spiritual gifts.

> There are different kinds of spiritual gifts, but the same Spirit is the source of them all. (1 Corinthians 12:4) NLT)

Greek = *pneumatikos*; spiritual

Greek = *charisma*; gift of grace, free gift

Spiritual gifts enable you to help other believers live, function, and serve.

> A spiritual gift is given to each of us so we can help each other. (1 Corinthians 12:7 NLT)

Help, Greek *sumpherō*; to be profitable; common good

> God has given each of you a gift from His great variety of spiritual gifts. Use them well to serve one another. (1 Peter 4:10 NLT)

Serve, Greek *diakoneō*; be an attendant; to wait upon.

It is also the Greek word rendered Deacon. The implication is that you are to humble yourself to be the attendant or servant of other Christians by using spiritual gifts.

Do you know your spiritual gifts? If not, you can discover them in this book.

12.

Three Types of Spiritual Gifts

THE FOUR LISTS of twenty spiritual gifts include the three types of spiritual gifts identified in the Bible. The three types of spiritual gifts are motivation, ministry, and manifestation.

MOTIVATION GIFTS

Motivation gifts are given by the Holy Spirit to motivate and encourage Christians to serve others.

Motivation gifts are given to encourage Christians to serve others.

The following is a list of the seven motivation gifts of Administration, Service, Mercy, Giving, Prophecy, Exhortation, and Teaching:

> For one person is given through the Spirit the message of wisdom, and another the message of knowledge according to the same Spirit, to another faith by the same Spirit, and to another gifts of healing by the one Spirit, to another performance of miracles, to another prophecy, and to another discernment of spirits, to another different kinds of tongues, and to another the interpretation of tongues. (1 Corinthians 12:8–10 NET)
>
> Here are some of the parts God has appointed for the church: first are apostles, second are prophets, third are teachers, then those

> who do miracles, those who have the gift of healing, those who can help others, those who have the gift of leadership, those who speak in unknown languages. Are we all apostles? Are we all prophets? Are we all teachers? Do we all have the power to do miracles? Do we all have the gift of healing? Do we all have the ability to speak in unknown languages? Do we all have the ability to interpret unknown languages? Of course not! He says believers are to use their spiritual gifts to help each other. (1 Corinthians 12:28–30 NLT)

Note: Prophecy, Teaching, and Apostle/Missionary are included in the following motivation gift description even though they are also in the ministry and manifestation lists in the Bible.

Administration

Those with this gift formulate, direct, and execute plans to fulfill God's purposes. They organize and supervise people in accordance with God-given purposes and long-term goals. They help people stay on task. They follow the visions and long-term goals created by those with the gift of Leadership.

Greek = *kubernēsis*; to guide, steer, pilot like a boat; to direct, govern

Many of the same ministry areas may be appropriate for individuals with the Administration and Leadership spiritual gifts. Administrators are better at organizing, planning, and executing details, while Leaders are better at creating and sharing a vision that encourages people's involvement. Both tend to be leaders in the local church. Many may also have the title of elder or pastor.

The following are typical behaviors and tendencies for believers with the motivation gift of Administration.

Typical Administration Strengths/Abilities:

- Excellent organization skills
- Define tasks and delegate work appropriately
- Work hard and expect others to do so
- Analytical and detail-oriented to develop plans and assign people
- Get the work done

Typical Administration Weaknesses:

- Disorganized in attempting to accomplish goals
- Uninvolved, apathetic in work attitude
- Not trustworthy in work ethic
- Arrogant and prideful about what they think they can accomplish
- Fearful about whether they can accomplish the work

Typical Misuse of Administrator Gift:

1. People are thought of as resources and not people
2. People are not as important as the work
3. Potentially a workaholic
4. Not a team player
5. Overwork themselves and others
6. Propel changes too fast instead of a gradual inclusion into the work environment

Note: They need to "slow down and smell the roses" in life.

Typical Temperament:
The most likely temperament for Administration is Doer. They may have the following temperament blend: Doer/Thinker.

Scripture References for Gift:
Some biblical references to the motivation gift of Administration follow: Nehemiah; 1 Corinthians 12:28; Acts 14:23; Acts 6:1–7 Luke 14:28–32.

Biblical Character with Gift:
One biblical person who demonstrates the motivation gift of Administration is: Nehemiah (book of Nehemiah).

Note: Some pastors, elders, and church board members may have this gift.

Service

Those with the gift recognize practical needs and joyfully assist in meeting those needs. Christians with this gift do not mind working behind the scenes.

Greek = *diakonia*; attendance as a servant, official service, ministering.

This is the same Greek word translated "deacon" in 1 Timothy 3:8–13 and Romans 16:1. The work of a deacon is described in Acts 6:1–6. The early church leaders in Jerusalem established the office of deacon to meet the practical needs of their church members.

Typical Service Strengths/Abilities:

- Always willing to serve
- Can be relied on to perform and finish work
- Loyal and dependable workers
- Work is done in a practical manner
- "Whatever-it-takes" attitude

Typical Service Weaknesses:

- Not involved and so unaware of needs
- Isolate themselves and can experience loneliness
- Focus on themselves may result in self-pity
- Want to do things their way, so may miss better ways of getting the work done
- Give up when work is not what they expect

Typical Misuse of Service Gift:

1. Home responsibilities are neglected
2. Accept too much work
3. Exhaust themselves and others
4. Help others when it is not God's will
5. Avoid standard procedures to get things done quickly
6. Loners who don't want help from others
7. Get sidetracked to other tasks and delay priority work

Typical Temperament:
The most likely temperament for Service is Doer.

What distinguishes the gift of serving from every Christian's duty to serve people? They immediately see and automatically respond with joy to fill a practical need. In contrast, it may take people without this gift some time to recognize the need, and if and how to address it.

Scripture References:
The following are some biblical references to the motivation gift of Service: Romans 12:7; Luke 23:50–54; Titus 3:14; Acts 9:36.

Biblical Characters with Gift:
The following biblical persons demonstrate the motivation gift of Service: Tabitha (Acts 9:36); Martha (Luke 10:38–42; John 12:2).

Mercy

Those with this gift consistently demonstrate acts of cheerful compassion. They aid the body by empathizing with people who are hurting (addressing spiritual, physical, and emotional needs). They respond to meet those needs. They help keep others aware of the needs of those hurting.

Greek = *Eleeo*; to feel empathy with the misery of another and to respond with action to bring them relief.

Typical Mercy Strengths/Abilities:

- Feel the hurt of others deeply
- Have caring hearts for others who are suffering
- Quickly respond to help others
- Demonstrate kindness and compassion for hurting people
- Very aware of the presence of hurting people around them

Typical Mercy Weaknesses:

- Lack of concern for the well-being of others
- Show partiality in helping others

- Harsh and rude in their attitude towards hurting people
- Angry at others who don't show mercy

Typical Misuse of Mercy Gift:

1. Felt pain of hurting people can get in the way of good decision-making
1. Decisions can be based on emotions instead of rational reasons
2. Can develop inappropriate affections for the opposite sex while helping them
3. Prefer not to associate with those who are insensitive to hurting people
4. Can blame God for allowing pain and hurt in others whom they want to see restored
5. Can be possessive with others they enjoy being with

Typical Temperament:
The most likely temperament for the gift of Mercy is Relator.

Scripture References:
The following are some biblical references that demonstrate the motivation gift of Mercy: Romans 12:6–8; Luke 7:12–15, 10:30–37; Matthew 1:18–24, 25:34–36; Mark 9:41; 1 Thessalonians 5:14; Colossians 3:12; James 2:13; Jude 1:22.

Biblical Character with Gift:
The following biblical person demonstrates the motivation gift of Mercy: Good Samaritan (Luke 10:29–34).

Note: People with the gifts of prophecy, giving, and mercy often gravitate toward prayer groups, especially intercessory prayer groups.

Giving

Those with this gift give freely and joyfully to the work and mission of Christ's Kingdom. They give generously and sacrificially of their resources of time, talent, and treasure.

Greek = *Metadidomi*; to give a share of, to impart

Typical Giving Strengths/Abilities:

- Find various ways to provide for needs of others
- Can be counted on
- Great stewards of what God has given them
- Giving heart and attitude
- Personally disciplined

Typical Giving Weaknesses:

- Can be extravagant in the use of resources
- Covet the wealth and possessions of others
- Late in providing for others
- Not grateful for what God has given them
- Give without prayer and careful attention to circumstances

Typical Misuse of Giving Gift:

1. Give too sparingly to their own family
2. This can cause family to resent gifts to others
3. Listen to unscriptural counsel on money management
4. Put pressure on people who have less to give
5. Fail to discern God's prompting for a gift
6. Judge those who don't use their funds well rather than advising them
7. Control people or ministries by their giving
8. Corrupt people by giving too much
9. Give to projects that do not benefit the lives of people

Typical Temperament:
The most likely temperament for giving is Doer. Possibly a Doer/Thinker blend.

Note: Interestingly, many givers have little money.

Scripture References:
The following Scripture demonstrates the motivation gift of Giving: Romans 12:8; 2 Corinthians 8:1–5, 9:2–15; John 12:3–8; Luke 3:11, 6:38, 21:1–4; Mark 4:24, 12:41–44; Matthew 6:1–4, 10:8; Ephesians 4:28.

Biblical Character with Gift:
The following believers demonstrate the motivation gift of Giving: Macedonian Churches (2 Corinthians 8:1–5).

Favorite Scripture: Philippians 4:19, *My God shall supply all your needs according to His riches in glory by Christ Jesus* (NASB).

Prophecy

Those with this gift proclaim the word of God with clarity and apply it fearlessly to strengthen, encourage, and comfort believers (1 Corinthians 14:3). They reveal and proclaim God's truths for understanding, correction, repentance, and edification. They can also proclaim God's message to convince unbelievers of God's reality.

Greek = *Propheteia*; pro = forth, pheine = to speak; to speak forth the mind and counsel of God.

Prophetic words can be forthtelling and foretelling.

Forthtelling: Speaking to announce God's will or intentions. Pronouncements may include warnings of God's judgment, calls for justice and righteousness, and concerns for the poor.

> Then Judas and Silas, both being prophets, spoke at length to the believers, encouraging and strengthening their faith. (Acts 15:32 NLT)

Foretelling: Predictions about events in the near or distant future.

> One of them named Agabus stood up in one of the meetings and predicted by the Spirit that a great famine was coming upon the entire Roman world. (This was fulfilled during the reign of Claudius.) (Acts 11:28 NLT)

Legitimate prophecy only comes from the Holy Spirit:

> Above all, you must realize that no prophecy in Scripture ever came from the prophet's own understanding, or from human initiative. No, those prophets were moved by the Holy Spirit, and they spoke from God. (2 Peter 1:20–21 NLT)

Note: Concern for truth is the heart of those with this gift. They see truth as of the utmost importance to people. They may think that if people are not living by God's truth, what eternal value do their lives have?

Typical Prophecy Strengths/Abilities:

- Often have the spiritual gift of Discernment to know the truth that others don't
- Don't compromise on presenting God's word
- Use the authority of Jesus as His prophets
- Willing to confront sin and call people to repentance
- Not afraid of people or circumstances
- Consult with other prophets to confirm that the message is from God

Typical Prophecy Gift Weaknesses:

- Deceitful in covering up truth
- Want their own way
- Don't do what they say (hypocrites)
- Impure in their personal lives
- Live in fear
- Argue about what is true instead of simply presenting it

Typical Misuse of Prophecy Gift:

1. Correcting people who are not their responsibility
2. Jumping to conclusions about words, actions, and motives of others
3. Judging and exposing offenders rather than restoring them
4. Cutting a person off who has failed to live by truth
5. Dwelling on the negative rather than the positive about truth
6. Lacking caution and tact in expressing opinions
7. Accusing others of deception if they do not fully reveal their faults

Typical Temperament:
The most likely temperament for prophecy is Doer. They may also be a Doer/Thinker blend.

Scripture References:
The following are biblical references to the motivation gift of Prophecy: Book of Isaiah; 1 Corinthians 12:7–11, 28–31, 13:2, 14:1–5, 24–25, 30–33, 37–40; Romans 12:6–8; Ephesians 4:11–13; 2 Peter 1:21; Acts 7:51–53, 10:9–17, 27–28, 11:27–28, 21:8–11, 26:24–29; 1 Thessalonians 1:5, 5:20; 1 Timothy 4:14.

Biblical Character with Gift:
The following biblical person demonstrates the motivation gift of Prophecy: Silas (Acts 15:32–33).

Note: Prophets may see visions, hear the voice of God, and so on We see this exemplified in the Old Testament prophets and Peter as a New Testament prophet.

Reminder: Before a prophet speaks—PRAY, PRAY, PRAY—to know if God wants them to speak!

Exhortation

Those with this gift encourage believers to be involved in and enthusiastic about the Lord's work. They motivate believers to serve Jesus Christ actively. They offer comfort, words of encouragement, hope, and reassurance to the discouraged, weak, and troubled.

Greek = *Paraklesis* = to call to a person, to walk with them; to urge and admonish to pursue a certain course of conduct.

Note: The Holy Spirit is referred to by Jesus as the *paraklētos* ; An intercessor, consoler, advocate, or comforter for believers.

Typical Exhortation Strengths/Abilities:

- Have a positive attitude on life
- Encourage and motivate others

- Support and affirm other people
- Reassure others that life with God is good
- Can be trusted
- Goal is for spiritual growth and a deeper relationship with God

Typical Exhortation Weaknesses:

- Self-centered
- Judgmental attitude toward others who don't serve as they think they should
- Make assumptions that may be inaccurate
- Careless and thoughtless in what they say to others
- Uninvolved, so don't let God use them
- Apathetic attitude about serving others

Typical Exhortation Misuses of the Prophecy Gift:

1. Raising the expectations of others prematurely
2. Can become overly self-confident
3. Taking family time to counsel others
4. Can burn out
5. Encouraging others to depend on them rather than God
6. Trusting visible results rather than a true change of heart in people
7. Neglecting proper emphasis on biblical doctrines
8. Can use Scriptures out of context to make a point

Typical Temperament:
The most likely temperament for the motivation gift of Exhortation is Relator. May also be an Influencer. They may have the Relator/Thinker temperament blend.

Scripture References:
The following are some biblical references to the motivation gift of Exhortation: Romans 12:8; 1 Thessalonians 2:11–12; John 14:1; 1 Timothy 4:13; 2 Timothy 1:16–18; Acts 4:32–37, 11:22–24, 14:22, 15:30–32; Ephesians 4:11–14; Hebrews 10:24–25.

Biblical Character with Gift:
The following biblical person demonstrates the motivation gift of Exhortation: Barnabas (Acts 4:36, 11:22–23, 13:1).

Teaching

Those with this understand and teach the Scriptures accurately. They instruct people in the truths and doctrines of God's Word for the purposes of building up, unifying, and maturing the body of Christ. They see truth as the foundation of life with God and of teaching His living word.

Greek = *Didasko*; to give instruction; to train

Typical Teaching Strengths/Abilities:

- Discipline themselves in life, in study, and in teaching
- Able to see what is true (may have the spiritual gift of Discernment)
- Open to being taught God's word if done by someone they respect
- View life from practical perspectives
- Many are detailed and analytical with the Thinker temperament (some are relational and not analytical)
- Articulate; speak to be understood
- Accurately teach the Bible
- Teach the Bible for practical application

Typical Teaching Weaknesses:

- Little self-control in their personal life
- Don't respect another teacher if they don't have a good biblical background and reputation as a qualified teacher
- Don't show reverent respect for God's word (it's just a resource for teaching)
- Too detailed and technical in their teaching (difficult to understand)
- Insufficient research might lead to incorrect conclusions for teaching
- Lack of consistency and persistence in preparations for teaching

Typical Teaching Misuses of the Gift of Teaching:

1. Become proud of their knowledge
2. Despise practical wisdom of uneducated people
3. Communicate skepticism toward their teachers and pastors, who they feel don't know God's word well
4. Criticize sound teaching because of technical flaws
5. Depend upon human reasoning rather than the Holy Spirit
6. Give information that lacks practical application (may not be interested in seeing changes inpeople's lives)
7. Bore listeners with details of research

Typical Temperament:
The most likely temperament for Teaching is Thinker. They may have a Thinker/Doer or Thinker/Relator temperament blend.

Scripture References:
The following biblical references demonstrate the motivation gift of Teaching: 1 Corinthians 4:17, 12:28; Matthew 4:23, 5:1–12, 28:19–20; Acts 18:24–28, 20:20–21; Romans 12:7; Ephesians 4:11–14; Hebrews 5:12; Colossians 3:16; Ecclesiastes 12:9–10.

Biblical Characters with Gift:
The following biblical person demonstrates the motivation gift of teaching: Apostle Paul (Acts 14:1–3).

MINISTRY GIFTS

Since the focus of this book is on motivation gifts, limited information is provided for the ministry gifts. Ministry gifts may be used by individuals in a formal ministry position or informally.

> There are different kinds of service, but we serve the same Lord. (1 Corinthians 12:5 NLT)

The five ministry gifts are listed in Ephesians 4:11 (NASB):

- Evangelism
- Pastor/Shepherd

- Apostle/Missionary
- Prophecy
- Teaching

Evangelism

Those with this gift have the ability to lead people to salvation in Christ. They build up the body of Christ by adding new believers to its fellowship.

Greek = *Evangelistes*; ev = well, angels, messengers; preacher of gospel

Scripture References:
The following Bible verses demonstrate the ministry gift of Evangelism: Matthew 28:16–20; Ephesians 4:11–16; Acts 2:36–40, 8:5–6, 26–40, 14:21, 21:8; 2 Timothy 4:5.

Biblical Characters with Gift:
The following biblical person demonstrates the ministry gift of Evangelism: Phillip (Acts 8:40, 21:8).

We see Philip referred to as an evangelist in the following verses:

> Philip, however, appeared at Azotus and traveled about, preaching the gospel in all the towns until he reached Caesarea. (Acts 8:40 NIV)
>
> Leaving the next day, we reached Caesarea and stayed at the house of Philip the evangelist, one of the Seven. (Acts 21:8 NIV)

Pastor /Shepherd

Those with this gift assume long-term responsibility for the leadership, spiritual care, protection, guidance, and teaching of a group of believers. They want Christians in their care to become more like Christ. This gift is not limited to pastors or church staff. Shepherds care for Christ's people through various formal and informal ministries. For example, Bible teachers can function as shepherds for their students.

Greek = *poimēn*; one who tends flocks; shepherd, pastor

Important: The role of a Pastor/Shepherd might imply they have the people-oriented Relator temperament. This is not always the case. Sometimes they have the task-oriented Doer temperament or a temperament blend.

Scripture References:
The ministry gift of Pastor/Shepherd is seen in the following verses: Ephesians 4:11–14;1 Timothy 4:6–16, 3:1–13; 2 Timothy 4:1–2; 1 Peter 5:1–3; John 10:1–18; Mark 6:34.

Biblical Character with Gift:
The following biblical person demonstrates the ministry gift of Pastor/Shepherd: Timothy (1 Timothy 4:6–16).

You see this in the Apostle Paul's instructions to Timothy, a young pastor follow:

> Teach these things and insist that everyone learn them. Don't let anyone think less of you because you are young. Be an example to all believers in what you say, in the way you live, in your love, your faith, and your purity. Until I get there, focus on reading the Scriptures to the church, encouraging the believers, and teaching them. Do not neglect the spiritual gift you received through the prophecy spoken over you when the elders of the church laid their hands on you. Give your complete attention to these matters. Throw yourself into your tasks so that everyone will see your progress. Keep a close watch on how you live and on your teaching. Stay true to what is right for the sake of your own salvation and the salvation of those who hear you. (1 Timothy 4:11–16 NLT)

Apostle

Those with this gift are sent to evangelize the unsaved and build new churches. They motivate local believers to look beyond the walls of their church to evangelize and carry out the Great Commission elsewhere. They may exercise leadership and oversight for multiple churches they start.

Note: The ministry of the Apostles in the early church included signs and wonders to validate the truth of their messages about Jesus Christ. This gift was not confined to the twelve apostles. The Apostle Paul (Acts 14:14) and several others had this title.

Note: The Apostle and Missionary both tend to follow similar approaches in establishing new churches. Both prefer to minister to unreached communities. The Apostle has a short-term focus in order to establish additional new churches. The missionary usually has a long-term focus to oversee the spiritual growth and well-being of new converts within a single church they start.

Greek = Apostolos; apo = from, stello = to send

Scripture References:
The following Bible verses demonstrate the ministry gift of Apostle: 1 Corinthians 12:28–31; Ephesians 4:11–16; 2 Corinthians 12:12; Matthew 10:1–8; Acts 2:42–44, 15:22–35; Galatians 2:6–8.

Biblical Characters with Gift:
The following biblical person demonstrates the ministry gift of Apostle: Apostle Paul (Galatians 2:6–8).

> And the leaders of the church had nothing to add to what I was preaching. (By the way, their reputation as great leaders made no difference to me, for God has no favorites.) Instead, they saw that God had given me the responsibility of preaching the gospel to the Gentiles, just as He had given Peter the responsibility of preaching to the Jews. For the same God who worked through Peter as the apostle to the Jews also worked through me as the apostle to the Gentiles." (Galatians 2:6–8 NLT)

Missionary

Much like apostles, those with this gift are sent to evangelize the unsaved and build new churches. They find it easy and exciting to adjust to a different culture or community. Missionaries experience great joy working with minorities, people from other countries, or those with distinct cultural differences. They have a strong desire to be part of fulfilling the Great Commission.

Note: There is no Greek word in the New Testament that identifies a missionary as a separate spiritual gift. The term is used to refer to the work of modern-day missionaries.

Scripture References:
The following Bible verses demonstrate the ministry gift of a Missionary: Ephesians 3:6–8; Mark 16:15; Acts 1:8, 8:4, 13:2–5, 22:21; Romans 10:14–15; 1 Corinthians 9:19–23.

Biblical Characters with Gift:
The following biblical person demonstrates the ministry gift of a Missionary: Apostle Paul (1 Corinthians 9:20–23).

> When I was with the Jews, I lived like a Jew to bring the Jews to Christ. When I was with those who follow the Jewish law, I too lived under that law. Even though I am not subject to the law, I did this so I could bring to Christ those who are under the law. When I am with the Gentiles who do not follow the Jewish law, I too live apart from that law so I can bring them to Christ. But I do not ignore the law of God; I obey the law of Christ. When I am with those who are weak, I share their weakness, for I want to bring the weak to Christ. Yes, I try to find common ground with everyone, doing everything I can to save some. I do everything to spread the Good News and share in its blessings. (1 Corinthians 9:20–23 NLT)

MANIFESTATION GIFTS

Since the focus of this book is on motivation gifts, limited information is provided for the manifestation gifts.

The Holy Spirit uses manifestation gifts to manifest, or demonstrate, His presence and work in and through believers.

The following is a list of the manifestation gifts:

> For one person is given through the Spirit the message of wisdom, and another the message of knowledge according to the same Spirit, to another faith by the same Spirit, and to another gifts of healing by the one Spirit, to another performance of miracles, to

> another prophecy, and to another discernment of spirits, to another different kinds of tongues, and to another the interpretation of tongues. (1 Corinthians 12:8–10 NET)

Note: This list does not include Helps, which is included in a duplicate list in 1 Corinthians 12:28.

Since I previously discussed the gifts of Prophecy, Teaching, and Apostle, they won't be described again.

- Helps (1 Corinthians 12:28)
- Faith
- Leadership
- Gifts of Healing
- Miracles
- Speaking in Tongues
- Interpretation of Tongues
- Word of Wisdom
- Word of Knowledge
- Discernment of Spirits

Helps

Those with this gift assist people in ministry, especially Christian leaders, so that the ministry of those helped is enhanced. They want to free up other believers so they can be more effective in ministry.

Greek = *antilēpsis*; to lay hold of, to support; relief, help, support.

Note: The distinction between the spiritual gifts of Service and Helps is not always clear regarding the types of work they may perform within the church.

The following is a brief distinction between the two gifts:

- Service: Usually seeks practical, hands-on activities
- Helps: Usually seeks activities they believe will free up other believers to be more effective in ministry

Scripture References:
The following Scripture identifies the manifestation gift of Helps: 1 Corinthians 12:28; Mark 15:40–41; Romans 16:1–2.

Biblical Characters with Gift:
The following biblical person demonstrates the manifestation gift of Helps: Phoebe (Romans 16:1–2).

Phoebe was known for her acts of helping and serving. She supported the faith community in any way possible. She was also a Deacon and regarded highly in the church. Paul commended her for the help she gave him, which allowed him to be more effective in his ministry. (Romans 16:1–2).

Faith

Those with this gift trust God to work beyond human capabilities. They encourage people to trust in God in the face of what appears to be insurmountable odds. They can envision the Holy Spirit at work and trust His leading, even without knowing what the results may be.

Important: Since faith is required to believe in the God of the Bible, many Christians mistakenly think they have the spiritual gift of Faith. As a manifestation gift, it is only given in circumstances determined to be necessary for the moment by the Holy Spirit. It may be a life-long gift from the Spirit.

Greek = *pistis*; trust, credence; moral conviction (of religious truth, or the truthfulness of God); assurance, belief

What is faith?

> Faith is the confidence that what we hope for will actually happen; it gives us assurance about things we cannot see. (Hebrews 11:1 NLT)

How great can this supernatural faith be?

> If I had such faith that I could move mountains. (1 Corinthians 13:2 NLT)

Scripture References:
The following Bible verses demonstrate the manifestation gift of Faith: 1 Corinthians 12:9; Acts 11:2–24, 27:23–25; Romans 4:18–21; Mark 5:25–34; 1 Thessalonians 1:8–10; Hebrews 11; 2 Timothy 1:5.

Biblical Character with Gift:
The following biblical person demonstrates the manifestation gift of Faith: Noah (Hebrews 11:7):

> It was by faith that Noah built a large boat to save his family from the flood. He obeyed God, who warned him about things that had never happened before. By his faith Noah condemned the rest of the world, and he received the righteousness that comes by faith. Hebrews 11:7 NLT)

Leadership

Those with this gift can cast vision, motivate, and direct people to accomplish God's purposes in a way that brings everyone together to achieve the goals for the glory of God.

Greek = *proistēmi*; (in rank) to preside, be over, rule.

Note: Many of the same ministries and service areas may be appropriate for individuals with the Administration and Leadership spiritual gifts. Administrators are better at organizing, planning, and executing details, while leaders are better at creating and sharing a vision for the ministry that encourages people's involvement.

Scripture References:
The following Scripture demonstrates the manifestation gift of Leadership: Romans 12:8; Galatians 2:2–6; 2 Timothy 4:1–5; 1 Timothy 3:1–13, 5:17; 1 Thessalonians 5:12; Hebrews 13:7, 13:17.

Biblical Character with Gift:
The following biblical person demonstrates the manifestation gift of Leadership: Spiritual leaders in Christ's church (Hebrews 13:17):

> Obey your leaders and submit to them, for they are keeping watch over your souls, as those who will have to give an account. Let

> them do this with joy and not with groaning, for that would be of no advantage to you. (Hebrews 13:17 ESV)

Word of Knowledge

Those with this gift know principles and truths that were previously unknown to them. These messages from the Holy Spirit promote the well-being and growth of the body of Christ. They may receive the Word of Knowledge while studying God's word or through an impartation of the Holy Spirit that is separate from study.

Greek = *Gnosis*; act of knowing, knowledge, science

Many of the same ministries and areas of service may be suitable for individuals with the spiritual gifts of the Word of Knowledge and the Word of Wisdom. Both speak God's word revealed by the Holy Spirit. Both are speaking forth something the person did not know beforehand.

Note: Sometimes the message from Word of Knowledge is similar to forth-telling in a prophetic utterance. Either way, the words are previously unknown to the speaker.

Scripture References:
The following biblical references demonstrate the manifestation gift of the Word of Knowledge: Ephesians 3:3–6; 1 Corinthians 12:7–11, 12:28, 14:6; Colossians 2:2–3; 2 Corinthians 11:6; Daniel 2:20–21; Proverbs 2:6, 9:10; Psalms 119:66; Jeremiah 3:15; 2 Chronicles 1:7–12.

Biblical Characters with Gift:
The following biblical person demonstrates the manifestation gift of the Word of Knowledge: Apostle Paul (Ephesians 3:3–6):

> As I briefly wrote earlier, God Himself revealed His mysterious plan to me. As you read what I have written, you will understand my insight into this plan regarding Christ. God did not reveal it to previous generations, but now by His Spirit He has revealed it to His holy apostles and prophets. And this is God's plan: Both Gentiles and Jews who believe the Good News share equally in the riches inherited by God's children. Both are part of the same body,

> and both enjoy the promise of blessings because they belong to Christ Jesus. (Ephesians 3:3–6 NLT)

Word of Wisdom

Those with this gift receive from the Holy Spirit spiritual truths that were previously unknown to them. They apply them in ways that benefit individuals and the church as a whole. With this wisdom, they can sort through opinions, ideas, and thoughts to discern truth. The Holy Spirit may also give the same believer a Word of Knowledge and a Word of Wisdom.

Greek = *Sophia*; wisdom (higher or lower, worldly or spiritual)

Many of the same ministries and areas of service may be suitable for individuals with the spiritual gifts of the Word of Knowledge and the Word of Wisdom. Both speak God's word revealed by the Holy Spirit. Both are speaking forth something the person with this gift did not know beforehand.

Scripture References:
The following Bible verses demonstrate the manifestation gift of the Word of Wisdom: 1 Corinthians 2:3–5, 6–13, 12:8; Acts 6:3–10; James 3:13–18; 2 Chronicles 1:7–11.

Biblical Characters with Gift:
The following biblical person demonstrates the manifestation gift of the Word of Wisdom: Stephen (Acts 6:1–6):

> But carefully select from among you, brothers, seven men who are well-attested, full of the Spirit and of wisdom, whom we may put in charge of this necessary task. But we will devote ourselves to prayer and to the ministry of the word." The proposal pleased the entire group, so they chose Stephen, a man full of faith and of the Holy Spirit, with Philip, Prochorus, Nicanor, Timon, Parmenas, and Nicolas, a Gentile convert to Judaism from Antioch. (Acts 6:1–6)

Discernment

Those with this gift know biblical truth and can differentiate between good and evil, truth and error, and right and wrong. They test people's messages and actions against the truth to protect and ensure the well-being of believers. They recognize people's true intentions. They help prevent confusion and false teaching from infiltrating Christ's church. They can identify the source as being from God, people, or demons.

Greek = *Diakrisia*; to investigate or judge

The following verses describe the gift of Discernment:

> Dear friends, do not believe every spirit, but test the spirits to see whether they are from God, because many false prophets have gone out into the world. This is how you can recognize the Spirit of God: Every spirit that acknowledges that Jesus Christ has come in the flesh is from God, but every spirit that does not acknowledge Jesus is not from God. This is the spirit of the antichrist, which you have heard is coming and even now is already in the world. (1 John 4:1–3 NIV)

> But we belong to God, and those who know God listen to us. If they do not belong to God, they do not listen to us. That is how we know if someone has the Spirit of truth or the spirit of deception. (1 John 4:6 NLT)

Note: The gift of Discernment may accompany a prophetic message.

Scripture References:
The following are biblical references that demonstrate the manifestation gift of Discernment: 1 Corinthians 2:9–16, 12:10; 1 John 4:1–6; John 16:6–15; Matthew 16:21–23; Acts 5:1–11, 8:9–23, 16:16–18; Romans 9:1.

Biblical Character with Gift:
The following biblical person demonstrates the manifestation gift of Discernment: Peter (Acts 8:9–23):

> Now for some time a man named Simon had practiced sorcery in the city and amazed all the people of Samaria. He boasted that he was someone great. . . . Simon himself believed and was baptized. And he followed Philip everywhere, astonished by the great signs and miracles he saw. When the apostles in Jerusalem heard that

> Samaria had accepted the word of God, they sent Peter and John to Samaria. When they arrived, they prayed for the new believers there that they might receive the Holy Spirit. . . . Then Peter and John placed their hands on them, and they received the Holy Spirit. When Simon saw that the Spirit was given at the laying on of the apostles' hands, he offered them money and said, "Give me also this ability so that everyone on whom I lay my hands may receive the Holy Spirit." Peter answered: "May your money perish with you, because you thought you could buy the gift of God with money! You have no part or share in this ministry, because your heart is not right before God. Repent of this wickedness and pray to the Lord in the hope that he may forgive you for having such a thought in your heart. For I see that you are full of bitterness and captive to sin." (Acts 8:9–23 NIV)

Healing, Miracles, Tongues

The spiritual gifts of Healing, Miracles, and Tongues have been the focus of debates among denominations and individuals. For example, some believe these gifts were only given during the time of the first-century apostles. They think they stopped with the death of the last apostle (John). However, there is no biblical evidence to support this idea. In fact, the following Scripture indicates otherwise:

> Love never fails. But where there are prophecies, they will cease; where there are tongues, they will be stilled; where there is knowledge, it will pass away. For we know in part and we prophesy in part, but when completeness comes, what is in part disappears. When I was a child, I talked like a child, I thought like a child, I reasoned like a child. When I became a man, I put the ways of childhood behind me. For now we see only a reflection as in a mirror; then we shall see face to face. Now I know in part; then I shall know fully, even as I am fully known. (1 Corinthians 13:8–12 NIV)

When will spiritual gifts come to an end? These verses indicate this occurs when Jesus Christ returns. Believers will see Him, and there will, therefore, be no need for any spiritual gift.

Important: Always seek answers in the Bible and through the guidance of the Holy Spirit for questions about anything in the Bible.

Healing

Those with this gift serve as human intermediaries through whom the Holy Spirit supernaturally heals illnesses and restores people's health. This healing can be physical, emotional, mental, or spiritual. The Holy Spirit can also heal through natural (non-supernatural) means, such as medicine, surgery, counseling, and so on.

Greek = *Iama*; to make whole (plural form, multiple gifts of healing)

Note: This is the only spiritual gift that uses the plural form, indicating there are many different ways the Holy Spirit will heal and restore people.

Scripture References:
The following are biblical references that demonstrate the manifestation gift of Healing: 1 Corinthians 12:7–11, 12:28–31; Acts 3:1–10, 9:32–35, 14:8–10, 28:7–10; James 5:14–16; Luke 9:1–2.

Biblical Character with Gift:
The following biblical persons demonstrate the manifestation gift of Healing: Apostles Peter and John (Acts 3:1–10):

> Now Peter and John were going up to the temple at the hour of prayer, the ninth hour. And a man lame from birth was being carried, whom they laid daily at the gate of the temple that is called the Beautiful Gate to ask alms of those entering the temple. Seeing Peter and John about to go into the temple, he asked to receive alms. And Peter directed his gaze at him, as did John, and said, "Look at us." And he fixed his attention on them, expecting to receive something from them. But Peter said, "I have no silver and gold, but what I do have I give to you. In the name of Jesus Christ of Nazareth, rise up and walk!" And he took him by the right hand and raised him up, and immediately his feet and ankles were made strong. And leaping up he stood and began to walk, and entered the temple with them, walking and leaping and praising God. And all the people saw him walking and praising God, and recognized him as the one who sat at the Beautiful Gate of the temple, asking for alms. And they were filled with wonder and amazement at what had happened to him. (Acts 3:1–10 ESV)

Miracles

Those with this gift serve as a human intermediary through whom the Holy Spirit performs acts of supernatural power. This supernatural action alters the natural world, authenticating the reality of the gospel and God.

Note: I have witnessed miracles and supernatural healings. I describe many of these in our first book, *Who Is This God? A Handbook for Life with Him*.

Greek words for the working of miracles:

Working = *energēma*; an effect, operation, working

Miracles = *Dunamis*; force (literally or figuratively), specifically miraculous power, ability

Scripture References:
The following Bible verses demonstrate the manifestation gift of Miracles: 1 Corinthians 12:7–11, 28–31; Mark 16:17–18; Acts 8:13, 9:36–42, 19:11–12, 20:7–12; Hebrews 2:4; Romans 15:17–19.

Biblical Character with Gift:
The following biblical person demonstrates the manifestation gift of Miracles: Philip (Acts 8:5–8):

> Philip, for example, went to the city of Samaria and told the people there about the Messiah. Crowds listened intently to Philip because they were eager to hear his message and see the miraculous signs he did. Many evil spirits were cast out, screaming as they left their victims. And many who had been paralyzed or lame were healed. So there was great joy in that city. (Acts 8:5–8 NLT)

Speaking in Tongues

Those with this gift praise and worship God supernaturally, through the Holy Spirit, in a language they have never learned. In their spirit, they receive and communicate a message that edifies and builds up believers (when correctly interpreted).

Greek = *glossa*; the tongue; by implication, a language (specifically a language not learned); Greek structure indicates diverse languages are available to be spoken.

The following verse suggests that there are numerous human languages, as well as those of angels. The Holy Spirit may use any of these to communicate a message unknown to the speaker.

> If I speak in the tongues of men and of angels. (1 Corinthians 13:1 ESV)

Important: Some churches are adamant that if a person does not speak in a tongue, they are not saved. However, the Bible clearly teaches that salvation in Christ has nothing to do with speaking in tongues.

> For by grace you have been saved through faith. And this is not your own doing; it is the gift of God, not a result of works, so that no one may boast. (Ephesians 2:8–9 ESV)

The following verse says not every believer will speak in a tongue or interpret a tongue:

> Now you are the body of Christ and individually members of it. And God has appointed in the church first apostles, second prophets, third teachers, then miracles, then gifts of healing, helping, administrating, and various kinds of tongues. Are all apostles? Are all prophets? Are all teachers? Do all work miracles? Do all possess gifts of healing? Do all speak with tongues? Do all interpret? (1 Corinthians 12:27–30 ESV)

Interestingly, when praying and singing in a tongue, the Holy Spirit engages the person's spirit rather than their mind.

> For if you have the ability to speak in tongues, you will be talking only to God, since people won't be able to understand you. You will be speaking by the power of the Spirit, but it will all be mysterious. (1 Corinthians 14:2 NLT)

> For if I pray in tongues, my spirit is praying, but I don't understand what I am saying. Well then, what shall I do? I will pray in the spirit, and I will also pray in words I understand. I will sing in the spirit, and I will also sing in words I understand. (1 Corinthians 14:14–15 NLT)

Tongues should only be spoken out loud in a group setting if there is someone to interpret. If there is no interpreter, the tongue should not be spoken.

> If any speak in a tongue, let there be only two or at most three, and each in turn, and let someone interpret. But if there is no one to interpret, let each of them keep silent in church and speak to himself and to God. (1 Corinthians 14:27–28 ESV)

Scripture References:
The following Bible verses demonstrate the manifestation gift of Speaking in Tongues: 1 Corinthians 12:7–11, 12:28–31, 14:1–40; Acts 2:1–12, 10:44–46, 19:1–7; Mark 16:17; Romans 8:26–27; Acts 2:4–8.

Biblical Character with Gift:
The following biblical person demonstrates the manifestation gift of Speaking in Tongues: Apostle Paul (1 Corinthians 14:18–19):

> I thank God that I speak in tongues more than all of you. Nevertheless, in church I would rather speak five words with my mind in order to instruct others, than ten thousand words in a tongue. (1 Corinthians 14:18–19 ESV)

Interpretation of Tongues

Those with this gift can supernaturally translate a message spoken in a language (tongue) unknown to them. The Holy Spirit enables them to understand and communicate the message.

Note: If a tongue is received and there is no interpretation, only the speaker benefits. If the tongue is interpreted, all those listening benefit.

Greek = *hermēneia*; translation, interpretation (of *glossa*, tongues or language)

Scripture References:
The following Bible verses demonstrate the manifestation gift of the Interpretation of Tongues: 1 Corinthians 12:7–11, 12:28–31, 14:1–40; Acts 2:4–8.

Biblical Character with Gift:
The following biblical persons demonstrate the manifestation gift of the Interpretation of Tongues: Some believers in the Corinthian church (1 Corinthians 14:5, 13).

We see this in the following verses:

> I wish you all spoke in tongues, but even more that you would prophesy. The one who prophesies is greater than the one who speaks in tongues, unless he interprets so that the church may be strengthened. (1 Corinthians 14:5 NET)

> So anyone who speaks in tongues should pray also for the ability to interpret what has been said. (1 Corinthians 14:13 NLT)

13.

Motivation Gifts Assessment

THE SPIRITUAL GIFTS Assessment lists all twenty spiritual gifts. You use it to rate how closely each gift statement describes you. To what degree does it reflect who you are? However, only motivation gifts are used to determine who you are. That's because you want to know which gifts motivate and inspire you to serve others.

HINTS FOR COMPLETING THE ASSESSMENT

The following hints may help you have more reliable assessment results.

Not Feeling Well Today?

If you are not feeling well or are under unusual stress, wait to complete the assessment until you are feeling better. These difficult circumstances may cause you to rate yourself differently than when you are feeling more like your usual self.

Don't take the motivation gift assessment when you are not feeling well.

Review Gift Descriptions First

I suggest reviewing the spiritual gifts descriptions before you complete the assessment. Having these fresh in your mind will help you decide how relevant a statement is to you.

Scoring

It's important to understand that this Spiritual Gifts Assessment is not about your spiritual maturity, nor about how good a Christian you think you should be. Its purpose is to help you identify the spiritual gifts the Holy Spirit has given you. Also, not all Christians have all the spiritual gifts.

You will rate yourself about how closely each statement reflects your typical self using the following scale: 2=Consistently true 1=Occasionally true 0=Never true.

You should expect a score of 2 for a statement about your strongest spiritual gifts. Your scores for the remaining statements will likely be 1 or 0. Your focus in the Analysis section is on your scores for the motivation gifts. Typically, people score high on only two or three of the motivation gifts. If you scored high on more than three, you might want to retake the assessment, knowing that one or more of these are not really who you are.

ASSESSMENT

Read each statement and write the number (2, 1, 0) in the column labeled "Answer." You are rating yourself on how closely a statement represents your typical self? How usually true is the statement about you?

	2=Consistently true, 1=Occasionally true, 0=Never true
Answer	**Statement**
	1. I enjoy bearing the responsibility for the success of tasks.
	2. Encouraging others is a high priority in my life.
	3. I have more faith in God in difficult situations than others.
	4. I give joyfully and liberally to people in financial need or to projects requiring financial support.

	2=Consistently true, 1=Occasionally true, 0=Never true
Answer	**Statement**
	5. I enjoy working behind the scenes to support the work of others and ministries.
	6. God has supernaturally healed people through my prayers, often by laying my hands on them.
	7. I am motivated to set goals and influence others to achieve them to advance God's work.
	8. Caring for hurting people is of the utmost importance to me.
	9. Sometimes when a person speaks in tongues, I understand what the Holy Spirit is saying.
	10. I am eager to communicate the Gospel with clarity and conviction so people can be saved.
	11. I am willing to assume long-term leadership, spiritual care, and guidance for a group of believers.
	12. I look for opportunities to explain and clarify the word of God to those who do not know or are confused about Scripture.
	13. I can readily distinguish between spiritual truth and error as well as good and evil.
	14. The Holy Spirit reveals things about people and situations, which I did not know beforehand.
	15. I can offer simple, practical biblical solutions in the midst of conflict or confusion.
	16. I like the idea of serving others to meet practical needs.
	17. I have spoken a message from the Holy Spirit in a language I have never learned.
	18. God has used me to do things supernaturally that were far beyond human or natural capabilities.
	19. I have a desire to speak messages directly from God that strengthen, encourage, and comfort believers.
	20. I am willing to leave comfortable surroundings and move somewhere else if it would enable me to share Christ with more people.
	21. I like to create detailed plans, organize, and lead people to achieve the goals of our church.
	22. I listen well and provide good advice to encourage and reassure others.
	23. I have confidence in God's continuing provision and help, even in difficult times, and especially when He has not yet provided.
	24. I manage my money well to free more of it to benefit other people, our church, and ministries.

	2=Consistently true, 1=Occasionally true, 0=Never true
Answer	**Statement**
	25. I enjoy doing routine tasks that support the needs of our church and ministries.
	26. I have a desire to pray for those who are physically or emotionally ill and ask God to heal them supernaturally.
	27. I find it easy to motivate others to follow through on ministry projects.
	28. I am drawn to help people regarded as undeserving or beyond help.
	29. If someone is speaking in tongues, the Holy Spirit sometimes gives me understanding of what was spoken.
	30. I speak about God's salvation through Jesus Christ, and see a positive response in those who are listening.
	31. I have a desire to oversee the ongoing spiritual growth of a group of Christians.
	32. I enjoy studying the Bible to learn God's truths and principles for my own life and to share with others.
	33. I can see through phoniness or deceit before it is evident to others.
	34. When reading or studying Scripture, the Holy Spirit reveals important biblical truths and principles to me.
	35. The Holy Spirit gives me biblical wisdom to help people, ministries, and the church.
	36. I am good at working with my hands and enjoy it when I have an opportunity.
	37. I have been given the ability to speak to God in a language that I have never learned
	38. The Holy Spirit has shown me what to pray for and answered my prayers so that supernatural results occurred in otherwise impossible situations.
	39. I am not afraid to speak boldly about evil in the world.
	40. I can adapt easily to other cultures, languages, and lifestyles, and would like to serve in foreign countries.
	41. I like to help groups of people and ministries in our church become more efficient and organized.
	42. I like motivating others to take steps for their spiritual growth and life as a Christian.
	43. I have a strong belief that God will work in circumstances in which success cannot be guaranteed by human effort.
	44. Influencing others for the Kingdom of God through finances is very important to me.

	2=Consistently true, 1=Occasionally true, 0=Never true
Answer	**Statement**
	45. I like to find things that can be done to help others, and often do them without being asked.
	46. The Holy Spirit speaks to me concerning people's illnesses so that I can pray for them to be healed.
	47. I can cast a vision for ministry that others want to follow and participate in.
	48. I hurt for others who are hurting, the sick, the poverty-stricken, and those in prison.
	49. I feel God wants to use me to benefit and bless others by interpreting tongues.
	50. I openly tell people that I am a Christian and want them to ask me about my faith.
	51. There are Christians whom I have been guiding for a long time with truth, encouragement, caring, and wisdom.
	52. I can communicate and teach Scripture in ways that cause others to learn and become motivated toward greater spiritual growth.
	53. Others tell me my insights into right and wrong are correct.
	54. The Holy Spirit reveals knowledge that is needed to help others in that moment.
	55. When faced with how to apply biblical truths, the Holy Spirit reveals solutions to me.
	56. I am willing to take an active part in helping with a project or practical need.
	57. When I speak in tongues in a group of believers, I believe it will benefit them when there is interpretation.
	58. God uses me to work miracles that defy the natural order so that His reality is manifested.
	59. Confronting someone with blatant sin in their life is not difficult for me, especially when I see others affected by it.
	60. I am attracted to ministries that start new churches, especially outside my local area.
	61. When I am participating in a group that is lacking organization, I want to take charge and organize it.
	62. I desire to counsel and help the confused, those guilty of sin, and the addicted.
	63. I have believed God when He spoke to me about the impossible and have seen it occur.
	64. I am confident that God will meet my needs, so I give sacrificially and consistently.

	2=Consistently true, 1=Occasionally true, 0=Never true
Answer	**Statement**
	65. I know that by assisting others, I have helped them become more effective in their ministries.
	66. When I pray for the sick, either I or they may feel sensations of tingling or warmth.
	67. I prefer to take the lead on tasks whenever necessary, even without being asked.
	68. I desire to work with those who have physical, mental, and emotional problems, to help alleviate their suffering.
	69. I have interpreted tongues with the result that a group of believers was strengthened in their faith, were encouraged, or comforted.
	70. I enjoy sharing the gospel with people I don't know.
	71. I am responsible for protecting Christians in my long-term spiritual care from dangerous influences.
	72. People have told me that I have helped them learn biblical truth in meaningful ways.
	73. I sense when situations are spiritually unhealthy.
	74. I receive insights about others while praying for them, even though I don't know them.
	75. I look for ways to apply biblical truths effectively to situations in my life.
	76. I enjoy routine work at the church that would seem boring to other people.
	77. Praying in the Spirit (tongues) is important to me.
	78. I know that God can miraculously alter circumstances through me.
	79. The Holy Spirit has revealed future things to me.
	80. I would like to present the gospel in a country whose culture and lifestyle are different than my own.

ANALYSIS

Write your answer values (2, 1, or 0) from the assessment under the matching statement number below. Write the total of the scores for each row in the "Total" column.

Note: Score teaching and prophecy as motivation gifts, not ministry or manifestation gifts. The assessment is for missionaries (not apostles), since we typically do not see apostles today.

Assessment Answer Values				Total	Spiritual Gift	Type Gift
1	21	41	61		Administration	Motiv.
2	22	42	62		Exhortation	Motiv.
4	24	44	64		Giving	Motiv.
8	28	48	68		Mercy	Motiv.
12	32	52	72		Teaching	Motiv.
16	36	56	76		Service	Motiv.
19	39	59	79		Prophecy	Motiv.
3	23	43	63		Faith	Man.
5	25	45	65		Helps	Man.
6	26	46	66		Healing	Man.
7	27	47	67		Leadership	Man.
9	29	49	69		Interpretation of Tongues	Man.
13	33	53	73		Discernment	Man.
14	34	54	74		Word of Knowledge	Man.
15	35	55	75		Word of Wisdom	Man.
17	37	57	77		Speaking in Tongues	Man.
18	38	58	78		Miracles	Man.
10	30	50	70		Evangelism	Min.
11	31	51	71		Shepherd/Pastor	Min.
20	40	60	80		Missionary (not Apostle)	Min.

Transfer your three highest-scored motivation gifts to your Profile.

PART F

Assessing Who You Are

14.

Cross-References

In this chapter, you will learn how spiritual gifts, temperament, and ministries are related.

LIVE BY THE SPIRIT

If you are living your life by the flesh, by the sinful characteristics of your temperament and spiritual gifts, it will be challenging to determine what ministry God is calling you to. The solution to both personal happiness and a greater ability to discern your ministry is to live by the Spirit. Living by the Spirit means that born-again believers allow the Holy Spirit to control their behavior and actions.

The following verses say that if you live by the Spirit, you will not fulfill the sinful desires of your flesh:

> But I say, live by the Spirit and you will not carry out the desires of the flesh. For the flesh has desires that are opposed to the Spirit, and the Spirit has desires that are opposed to the flesh, for these are in opposition to each other, so that you cannot do what you (Galatians 5:16–17 NET)

You will also serve others with greater spiritual life and power, building them up spiritually by the Spirit.

TEMPERAMENT AND SPIRITUAL GIFTS CROSS-REFERENCE

Your God-given natural temperament harmonizes with your spiritual gifts and natural talents. God wants everything He gives you in the spiritual and natural realms to be available to Him to accomplish His purposes.

The following are possible spiritual gifts associated with the four temperaments. While some of these may seem obvious, others are more speculative. However, God will provide any combination of temperament and spiritual gifts He desires for His purposes.

Temperament	Possible Spiritual Gifts (Motivation in italics)
Relator	*Mercy*, *Exhortation*, *Teaching*, Helps, Missionary, Healing, Giving
Doer	Evangelism, *Administration*, Leadership, *Giving*, Faith, Helps, Interpretation of Tongues, Speaking in Tongues, Discernment, *Service*, Miracles, *Prophecy*, Missionary, Pastor/ Shepherd
Thinker	*Administration*, *Exhortation*, Faith, Leadership, Interpretation of Tongues, Speaking in Tongues, Pastor/ Shepherd, *Teaching*, Discernment, Word of Knowledge, Word of Wisdom
Influencer	*Exhortation*, Faith, *Giving*, Leadership, Evangelism, Pastor/Shepherd, Word of Knowledge, Word of Wisdom, Speaking in Tongues, Interpretation of Tongues, Missionary

TEMPERAMENT AND MINISTRY CROSS-REFERENCE

The following is a cross-reference between the four temperaments and possible ministries. The cross-reference is based upon a ministry's focus on people or tasks.

Doer

Best types of ministries: task-oriented ministries that require little supervision and detail.

Biblical example of temperament: Peter

Influencer

Best types of ministries: One-to-many ministries, such as public speaking, outreach, mission field, and church planting.

Biblical example of temperament: Apollos

Thinker

Best types of ministries: Ministries requiring details and analysis, such as artists and musicians.

Biblical example of temperament: Paul

Relator

Best types of ministries: One-to-one ministries, such as educators, mediators, counselors, and mentors.

Biblical example of temperament: John

SPIRITUAL GIFTS AND MINISTRY CROSS-REFERENCE

God has also equipped every Christian with spiritual gifts that can be more effective in specific ministries.

> Just as our bodies have many parts and each part has a special function, so it is with Christ's body. We are many parts of one body, and we all belong to each other. In His grace, God has given us different gifts for doing certain things well. (Romans 12:4–6 NLT)

Spiritual Gifts and Ministry Cross-Reference

The following indicates how spiritual gifts can benefit specific ministries. I have listed these by the type of spiritual gift.

Note: These are my opinions based on experience with spiritual gifts and ministries.

Note: I don't repeat the cross-references for Teaching, Prophecy, and Apostle (Missionary) gifts.

Motivation Gifts

Administration:

- Adult ministry
- Youth ministry
- Children's ministry
- Church teams
- Church planting
- Ministry development
- Governing board
- Finance
- Business management
- Pastor/Elder
- Evangelism and outreach
- Small groups
- Discipleship
- Missions
- Conferences/Seminars

Prophecy:

- Pastor/Elder
- Missions

- Governing board
- Intercessory prayer
- Evangelism and outreach

Teaching:

- Adult ministry
- Youth ministry
- Children's ministry
- Counseling
- Small groups
- Support groups
- Bible study classes (including Sunday School)
- Conferences/Seminars
- Discipleship

Exhortation:

- Hospital/Home/Institution visitation
- Counseling
- Small groups
- Discipleship
- Worship and music
- Governing board
- Intercessory prayer
- Prayer chain
- Teaching
- Adult ministry
- Youth ministry
- Children's ministry

Service:

- Church Building/Grounds maintenance
- Church office support

- Communications and media support
- Activities/Events support (including preparation, cooking, clean-up, and so on)
- Deacon
- Greeters/Ushers
- Child care and nursery worker
- Computer ministry
- Sports ministry support

Giving:

- Finance
- Capital fundraising campaigns
- Counseling
- Missions
- Governing board
- Adult ministry
- Youth ministry
- Children's ministry

Mercy:

- Home/Hospital/Institution visitation
- Counseling
- Discipleship
- Missions
- Adult ministry
- Youth ministry
- Children's ministry
- Intercessory prayer
- Prayer chain
- Specialty ministries (such as the mentally impaired)
- Support groups

- Small groups
- Healing ministry

Ministry Gifts

Missionary:

- Governing board
- Church planting
- Discipleship
- Church planting (targeting people in other cultures)
- Intercessory prayer
- Missions
- Pastor/Elder
- Teacher
- Evangelism and outreach

Evangelist:

- Evangelism and outreach
- Governing body
- Church planting (targeting non-believers)
- Intercessory prayer
- Pastor/Elder
- Newcomers events
- Breadwinners
- Home groups
- Drama club
- Prayer chain
- Sports ministry
- Vacation Bible School

Pastor (Shepherd)/Elder:

- Pastor/Elder
- Teaching
- Missions
- Governing board
- Counseling
- Ministry team leader
- Discipleship
- Missions
- Intercessory prayer
- Evangelism and outreach
- Ministry development
- Church planting
- Home churches
- Small groups

Manifestation Gifts

Faith:

- Hospital/Home/Institution visitation
- Counseling
- Discipleship
- Intercessory prayer
- Prayer chain
- Church teams
- Worship and music
- Missions
- Support groups
- Small groups

- Adult ministry
- Youth ministry
- Children's ministry

Leadership:

- Adult ministry
- Youth ministry
- Children's ministry
- Church teams
- Church planting
- Ministry development
- Governing board
- Finance staff
- Business management
- Pastor/Elder
- Evangelism and outreach
- Small groups
- Discipleship
- Missions

Helps:

- Church Building/Grounds maintenance
- Church office support
- Communications and media support
- Activities/Events support (including preparation, cooking, clean-up, and so on)
- Pastor/Elder
- Evangelism and outreach
- Deacon
- Greeters/Ushers
- Child care and nursery worker

- Computer ministry
- Sports ministry support

Miracles:

- Missions
- Specialty ministries
- Intercessory prayer
- Prayer chain
- Evangelism and outreach
- Worship and music
- Healing ministry
- Support groups
- Small groups

Healing:

- Specialty ministries
- Counseling
- Intercessory prayer
- Prayer chain
- Evangelism and outreach
- Worship and music
- Healing ministry
- Support groups

Word of Knowledge and Word of Wisdom:

- Counselor
- Discipleship
- Support groups
- Small groups
- Governing board
- Intercessory prayer

- Prayer chain
- Worship and music
- Healing ministry
- Specialty ministries

Speaking in Tongues and Interpretation of Tongues:

- Counselor
- Discipleship
- Evangelism and outreach
- Support groups
- Small groups
- Intercessory prayer
- Prayer chain
- Worship and music
- Healing ministry
- Specialty ministries

Discernment:

- Counselor
- Discipleship
- Evangelism and outreach
- Support groups
- Small groups
- Governing board
- Intercessory prayer
- Prayer chain
- Worship and music
- Healing ministry
- Specialty ministries

15.

Assessments

THIS CHAPTER ENABLES you to envision who you are and how you function through assessments.

NATURAL GIFTS AND TALENTS ASSESSMENT

What are three natural gifts and talents you received when you were born physically into this world? Some examples could include sewing, sports, math, hospitality, baking, and landscaping.

1.
2.
3.

Transfer these to your Profile.

Your natural gifts and talents can be used by God for His purposes.

EXPERIENCES AND EDUCATION ASSESSMENT

As you reflect on your life, you may discover that you have education and experiences that can help you in ministry. Your education may enable you to perform certain types of work, contribute to organizations, and be involved in specific ministries and services. Some examples of education might be: business management, psychology, computer graphics, and so on. Your experiences may allow you to be more effective in certain types of work and specific ministries. Examples of such experiences might include the military, teaching, and nursing home care.

Education

Write a brief description of how your education has benefited you in ministry.

Experiences

Write a brief description of how your experiences have benefited you in ministry.

Transfer these statements to your Profile.

SPIRITUAL MATURITY ASSESSMENT

You will use the Discipleship Pathway for this assessment of spiritual maturity. Consider how your spiritual maturity might benefit your work, home life, and Christian ministry.

In the following Scriptures, God says that He wants His people to become spiritually mature:

> This will continue until we all come to such unity in our faith and knowledge of God's Son that we will be mature in the Lord, measuring up to the full and complete standard of Christ. (Ephesians 4:13 NLT)

> Solid food is for those who are mature, who through training have the skill to recognize the difference between right and wrong. (Hebrews 5:14 NLT)

Discipleship Pathway

The discipleship pathway describes how a person transitions from a non-believer in Jesus Christ to a Christian leader.

Discipleship Pathway Assessment

We are all at different stages of spiritual growth. The purposes of this assessment are to determine your current level of spiritual maturity and how God might use you. For example, if you are at the Spiritual Leader stage, God can use you to lead, guide, and nurture others.

A typical discipleship pathway might include the following stages.

Inquirer: Non-Christian, but interested in learning more about Jesus Christ and the Christian life. This person is still inquiring, probing, and investigating who Jesus Christ is and what the Christian life is really like. Spiritual life from God has not yet begun. (Biblical example: Lydia)

Young Christian: A newly born-again Christian just learning about God and Christianity. They are beginning to develop a personal relationship with Jesus Christ. This might also be a person who has been a Christian for some time but is only now discovering spiritual life with Jesus Christ. Spiritual maturity at this level is reflected in excitement and joy as one develops a personal relationship with Jesus Christ. (Biblical example: Timothy)

Growing Christian: A committed Christian who has been regularly worshiping, learning about, and obeying Jesus Christ as Lord and Savior. They have a stable and confident personal relationship with Jesus Christ. The fruit of the Spirit is evident in this believer's life. They are routinely using their spiritual gifts to serve others. They consistently apply God's living word to ministry and their personal life. They seek the Holy Spirit to work in and through them. (Biblical example: Silas)

Spiritual Leader: A strong and mature Christian well-grounded in the word of God and consistently living by the Spirit of God. They do this through the strength of a long-standing, well-tested personal relationship with Jesus Christ. They know the God of the Bible. This Christian routinely provides spiritual nurturing, training, and guidance to Young and Growing Christians. Their goal is to help them live by the Spirit and develop a more profound commitment and enjoyment in their relationship with Jesus Christ. This Christian may also nurture Inquirers to help bring them to salvation in Jesus Christ. Spiritual maturity at this level is reflected in the gentle spirit of Christ that inspires other Christians to desire to know Him, learn His word, and live a consistent spiritual life. (Biblical example: Apostle Paul)

Spiritual Movement

Spiritual movement refers to the process by which a person transitions from one spiritual stage to the next along the pathway.

Reasons for moving from Inquirer to Young Christian:

- The church community may be something they want to be a part of
- Seeking spiritual guidance
- Believe God and Jesus exist
- Holy Spirit is inviting the Inquirer to know Jesus Christ and convicting them of sin

Reasons for moving from Young Christian to Growing Christian:

- Responding to the Holy Spirit's invitation to accept Christ as Savior and Lord
- Looking for ways to enjoy the community of other believers
- Believe no one can earn salvation
- Study Scripture to know the God of the Bible better and how to live the Christian life

Reasons for moving from Growing Christian to Spiritual Leader:

- Want their beliefs, attitudes, and emotions to reflect the character of Christ
- Strive to surrender their entire life to Christ

- Study Scripture to apply to themselves and to share with others
- The Holy Spirit empowers them to share the gospel and lead people to salvation in Christ

Analysis

Consider these four levels of spiritual maturity and review the depth of your personal relationship with Jesus Christ. Consider the condition of your inner character and your outward behavior. Pray and ask the Lord to confirm the depth and breadth of your personal relationship with Him, as well as your level of spiritual maturity.

Circle the stage of your current spiritual maturity:

- Inquirer
- Young Christian
- Growing Christian
- Spiritual Leader

Transfer your spiritual maturity stage to your Profile.

MINISTRY ASSESSMENTS

The following might help you identify ministries for which you are suited:

- Typical Ministries
- Ministry Passion Assessment
- Ministry Availability Assessment

TYPICAL MINISTRIES

There are typical ministries that most churches utilize to support their congregation and activities. Churches may have different names for their ministries and perform them in slightly different ways, but they are essentially the same in their overall purpose.

Worship Service:

- Sound/Audio
- Computer Graphics
- Lighting
- Music
- Camera
- Communion
- Technology
- Prayer Team

People Encounter:

- Greeter
- Hospital Visitation
- Nursing Home Visitation
- Card Ministry (for example, get well, happy birthday)
- Military Ministry
- Prayer Blankets
- Tutoring Ministry
- Grief Ministry
- Divorce Recovery Ministry
- Wedding Coordination
- Pre-Marriage Ministry
- Marriage Ministry
- School Supplies Ministry (for example, backpacks for school children)
- Transportation
- Intercessory Prayer
- Newcomers Events Committee
- Prayer Chain
- Sports Ministry

Christian Education:

- Vacation Bible School
- Youth Ministry
- Children's Ministry
- Special Needs Ministry
- Womens Ministry
- Mens Ministry
- Adult Sunday School
- Home Groups
- Conferences/Seminars

Outreach:

- Evangelism
- Missions Engagement and Support
- Community Engagement

Church Support:

- Grounds Keeping
- Church Repairs
- Church Cleaning
- Library
- Office Assistance
- Safety Team
- Money Counting
- Auditing Church Books

Church Leadership:

- Elder
- Pastor
- Deacon
- Yoke Fellow
- Ministry Leader

Use the above information to complete your Ministry Passion Assessment.

MINISTRY PASSION ASSESSMENT

How strongly do you feel about serving specific people and ministries? One way God provides direction is through your feelings and heart's desires.

Your passion for ministry comes from God.

To discover your passion most effectively, assume you have no limitations, such as time, geographic location, job, money, or skill.

Note: If needed, apply logic and reason to be realistic about what is a possible ministry.

Assessment:

1. When you think of possible ministries, what comes to mind? For example, unwed mothers, persecuted Christians, people suffering from illness, baby Christians struggling in their faith, unbelievers in second and third-world countries, and so on. Describe your passion here.

2. What type of people do you especially enjoy doing things for? Describe your passion here.

Helpful hint: Who is your Christian role model, and what spiritual gifts do you see in them?

Person:
Why:

Analysis:

Note: Look for an underlying continuity in your responses. See how your responses point to a passion for specific people and ministries.

Transfer your passion for serving specific people and ministries to your Profile.

MINISTRY AVAILABILITY ASSESSMENT

You have learned that God has equipped you to serve in His Kingdom. To serve, you must make yourself available.

The following verse says believers are to serve each other with what God has given us:

> From him the whole body, joined and held together by every supporting ligament, grows and builds itself up in love, as each part does its work. (Ephesians 4:16).

Assessment:

As you complete this assessment, realistically determine how much time you can commit to serving. Commit this amount of time. If you believe your current available time is inadequate, ask God to help you alter your life so more time is available.

The following questions will assist you in determining your ministry availability:

1. Do I regularly work more than a 40–50-hour work week at my job? Circle your answer below.

   Yes

   No

What specifically will you do to adjust your work schedule so that you can spend more time in ministry?

2. Does each member of your family receive at least half an hour of your time most days of the week? Circle your answer below.

   Yes

   No

   What specifically will you do to spend more time with each member of your family (1 Timothy 5:8)?

3. Are you spending at least one-half hour each day in prayer and Bible study? Circle your answer below.

   Yes

   No

   What specifically will you do to spend more time in prayer and Bible study each day?

4. Are you getting adequate rest, exercise, and relaxation to maintain stable physical and mental health? Circle your answer below.

   Yes

   No

   What specifically will you do to spend more time maintaining stable physical and mental health?

Analysis:

Consider your responses and realistically determine the average number of hours a week you can commit to service.

Estimate of average ministry hours per week:

Transfer the weekly hours to your Profile.

WRAPPING MINISTRY ASSESSMENT UP

Ministry Consultation

You may also want to contact your pastor, an elder, or a ministry leader to identify possible places to serve. You might ask them to allow you the time to try out several ministries before committing to one. See how you enjoy the ministry and whether others perceive it as a good fit for you.

Transfer your consultation feedback to your Profile.

Let's review your Profile to identify patterns and discover more about who you are and where God is calling you to serve.

Profile

Your Profile is a snapshot of who God has created you to be and how He has prepared you to serve.

YOUR PROFILE

I believe the following indicates how God has created and developed me to serve Him and others.

Temperament

Circle what you believe to be your temperament. Remember that many people are a blend of two or more temperaments, so circle those in your blend.

- Doer
- Influencer
- Relator
- Thinker

Motivation Gifts Assessment: Highest Three Scores

Write your three highest motivation gifts here.

- First
- Second
- Third

Top Three Natural Gifts and Talents

Write your three highest natural gifts and talents here.

- First
- Second
- Third

Experiences and Education

Write your education and experiences here.

Education:

Experiences:

Spiritual Maturity Assessment

The Discipleship Pathway can provide a snapshot of your current spiritual maturity. Circle where you are on the pathway.

Note: If you are transitioning between two stages, circle both.

- Inquirer
- Young Christian
- Growing Christian
- Spiritual Leader

Ministry Passion Assessment

Describe the ministries and people you have a passion to serve.

Ministry Availability Assessment

Write down the number of average hours per week you can allocate to ministry.

Ministry Consultation Feedback

Write down the feedback you received from your ministry consultation(s).

Conclusion

I believe the ministries and people God is calling me to serve at this time are as follows:

- First
- Second
- Third

Prayer to Know God

I'M A GOOD PERSON

Sometimes, people ask, "Isn't being a good person enough to get into Heaven?" But we must ask ourselves the following questions: "How good is good enough?" and "Whose measuring stick for goodness are we using?" Have you ever done anything wrong in your life? If so, you are not perfect and, therefore, not good enough to enter God's perfect Heaven.

> Your eyes are too pure to look on evil; you cannot tolerate wrong-doing. (Habakkuk 1:13 NIV)

> You therefore must be perfect, as your heavenly Father is perfect. (Matthew 5:48 ESV)

No One Can Earn Salvation

No one is perfect enough to live in God's holy presence. Every person (no matter how nice they are) has said, thought, and done things that displease God. He refers to these behaviors as "sin."

The Greek word translated "sin" is sometimes understood as "missing the mark" of God's perfection. Perhaps it's better understood if we say sin is active or passive rebellion against God.

> For everyone has sinned; we all fall short of God's glorious standard. (Romans 3:23 NLT)

What about the person who says, "I have always been a Christian." Can this be true? No, it's not true. Instead, the opposite is true.

> And remember that those who do not have the Spirit of Christ living in them do not belong to Him at all. (Romans 8:9 NLT)

> There is no judgment against anyone who believes in Him. But anyone who does not believe in Him has already been judged for not believing in God's one and only Son. (John 3:18 NLT)

Note: The Holy Spirit dwells within people only when they commit their hearts and lives to Jesus as Savior and Lord.

There Is No Hope without Jesus Christ

The following verses describe a person's spiritual condition without Jesus Christ.

> In those days you were living apart from Christ. You were excluded from citizenship among the people of Israel, and you did not know the covenant promises God had made to them. You lived in this world without God and without hope. (Ephesians 2:12 NLT)

> For the sinful nature is always hostile to God. It never did obey God's laws, and it never will. That's why those who are still under the control of their sinful nature can never please God. (Romans 8:7–8 NLT)

I heard a pastor say that you "must step across the line" to choose to leave your old, condemned life and accept God's new, eternal life in Christ. It's the most important decision you will ever make.

Some born-again followers of Jesus cannot state a specific date or event when they committed their lives to Him. But they know in their hearts they have done this.

> For it is by believing in your heart that you are made right with God, and it is by confessing with your mouth that you are saved. (Romans 10:10 NLT)

Your Prayer to Know God

Please pray this from your heart to enter an eternal relationship with the Father, His Son, Jesus Christ, and the Holy Spirit.

> Dear God, thank you for loving me and caring about me. Thank you for wanting me to be with you forever and for sending Jesus to be my Savior and Lord. I believe that Jesus died on the cross, that He was dead and buried, and was raised back to life by your supernatural power, according to the Scriptures.
>
> Please forgive me for all my sins against you and people. I commit to live under the authority and rule of Jesus Christ as my Savior and Lord.
>
> Thank you, Father, for sending your Holy Spirit to live within me to guide, help, and teach me. I know that I now have eternal life with you.

If you sincerely prayed the above from your heart, you are now a born-again Christian, a follower of Jesus Christ. The Holy Spirit is living within you. Welcome to the eternal family of God!

You now have the following relationship with each person of the Trinity. You are a:

- Child of your Father God (Galatians 3:26)
- Disciple and brother/sister of Jesus Christ (Mark 3:35)
- Temple in which the Holy Spirit lives (1 Corinthians 6:19)

Glossary

THE FOLLOWING GLOSSARY PROVIDES the meaning of key terms in this book.

Assessments: Help you discover who you are and how God has equipped you to serve.

Born-Again: Jesus said that everyone must be born-again to enter the Kingdom of God (John 3:3). This occurs immediately when the Holy Spirit comes to live within people when they commit their hearts and lives to Jesus Christ as Savior and Lord.

Conscience: The existence of conscience is part of your human nature. God has given every person a conscience to discern right from wrong. However, you can be taught to believe something is right when it is actually wrong. Since you are not perfect, and neither are their cultures, your sense of right and wrong can be modified to be contrary to God. If in doubt, always look it up in your guidebook of truth, the Bible. The saying, "Let your conscience be your guide," can be misleading. Instead, ask the Holy Spirit to be your guide.

Creation: The Bible describes creation in the first two chapters of the Old Testament book of Genesis. The first verse in the Bible says that the Triune God existed before creation, *In the beginning, God created the heavens and the earth* (Genesis 1:1 ESV).

Cross-References: Enable you to see how you compare across different variables.

Discipleship Pathway: Description of how you transition from a non-believer in Jesus Christ to a Christian leader.

Filled with the Spirit: Means you are embracing the Holy Spirit completely and allowing Him to control you.

Fruit of the Spirit: Part of your visible new nature resulting from spiritual growth.

Great Commission: The Lord Jesus Christ's mandate for His followers to go into the world and preach and teach the gospel. The results are that non-believers will be saved and trained to know God and live their lives for Him. Churches may be planted as a result.

Heal (Healing): God can supernaturally heal a person of physical, mental, and emotional illnesses. He can also give insight to people and healthcare professionals that can help restore a person's health naturally. Being rescued from eternal condemnation by accepting Jesus is spiritual healing.

Human Need: Something that must be fulfilled in the physical, psychological, and social context of human existence. A severe lack can lead to physical death.

Human Want: Not something that is required for survival. It's a preference, a desire for something in the physical, psychological, or social realm that brings pleasure to the person.

Manifestation Gift: Used by the Holy Spirit as a way to manifest, or demonstrate His presence and work in and through you.

Ministry Gift: Used by the Holy Spirit to provide a means for you to serve in formal and informal ways.

Motivation Gift: Used by the Holy Spirit to motivate and inspire you to serve.

Natural Gifts and Talents: Given by God to you at physical birth.

Natural Temperament: God has a purpose and plan for your life. This includes a specific temperament given at physical birth.

New Nature (Believers): When youcommit your heart and life to Jesus Christ, you become a member of God's eternal family. You are born-again by the Holy Spirit. At that moment, He gives you a new nature that matures over time into the nature of Jesus Christ. However, a lack of spiritual purpose, desire, and discipline to grow spiritually can prevent this growth. As a result, the old nature will continue to dominate.

Old Nature (All People): When you are physically born, you have a self-centered, old nature. Your old nature never goes away. Only being born-again by the Holy Spirit can give a you a new nature centered on Jesus Christ.

Renewed Mind: Your mind as a Christian is being transformed by God's living word into the mind of Christ.

Sentient: Means you are capable of sensing what is occurring within and around you. You are conscious of your environment and can thoughtfully respond to it.

Spirit, Soul, and Body: God created you in His image. You have a spirit, soul, and body. When you committed your heart and life to Jesus Christ, the Holy Spirit came to live within you, and you were born-again. When this occurs, your spirit (which was dead to God before salvation) is made alive to God. It's through your spirit that you can experience and communicate with God. Your soul is composed of emotions, desires, thoughts, motivations, and conscience. Your soul is how you interact with people and life in the natural world. The physical body allows you to live within the physical world God created.

Spiritual Gift: At spiritual birth, the Holy Spirit gave you spiritual gifts to assist you in fulfilling God's purpose for your life in His Kingdom.

Spiritual Growth: Process of being transformed into the character and image of Jesus Christ. Having the character and spiritual nature of Jesus Christ is your goal in this growth process. The fruit of the Spirit is the result of spiritual growth.

Spiritual Maturity: As you pursue your eternal relationship with God, you grow and become mature followers of Jesus.

Survival Need: Required for physical existence to continue.

Bibliography

Anderson, Neil T. *Living Free in Christ, The Truth about Who You Are and How Christ Can Meet Your Deepest Needs.* Ventura: Regal Books, 1993.

Blackaby, Henry, and Mel. *What's so spiritual about your gifts.* Sisters: Multnomah Publishers, 2004.

Harris, Guy, and Kevin Eikenberry. "Disc Personality Testing." (The Kevin Eikenberry Group). Accessed 2/2/2026, https://discpersonalitytesting.com.

Hodge, Kimball. *A Mind Renewed by God, Forever Changing the Way You Think and Live.* Eugene: Harvest House Publishers, 1998.

Home Missions Staff. *Discover Your Gifts Workbook.* Third, revised edition. Grand Rapids: Church Development Resources, 1983.

Jackson, John Paul. *Needless Casualties of War.* Fort Worth: Streams Publishing, 1999.

Moore, Gary L. *Life in the Spirit Seminar.* Goodlettsville: Aldersgate Renewal Ministries, 2003.

Nelson, Mary, Roach, Steve, Tardif, Cathy (writers). *Spiritual Passion, Using My Gifts in Christian Community.* Serendipity Small Group Plus Series. Littleton: Serendipity House, 2000. (Note: Serendipity House Publishing was acquired by Lifeway Christian Resources in 2002.)

Thurman, Chris. *The Lies We Tell Ourselves, Overcome Lies Like These and Experience the Emotional Health, Intimate Relationships, and Spiritual Fulfillment You've Been Seeking.* Nashville: Thomas Nelson, Inc., 1999.

Wikipedia. "Four temperaments." Accessed 2/2/2026, https://fourtemperaments.com/test.

www.ingramcontent.com/pod-product-compliance
Lightning Source LLC
La Vergne TN
LVHW020632100826
845148LV00012B/2157

* 9 7 9 8 3 8 5 2 7 7 3 9 1 *